The Digital Future of Hospitality

"Whether as fact or fantasy, the rhetoric of the digital world is riddled with invocations of hospitality, but to what ends and with what effects? What happens when a traditionally humanist concept incorporates or adapts itself to what some call the posthuman? What kind of home is the homepage, what shelter is provided by airbnb? Is the hacker friend or enemy? How much of FemTech is still just Tech, producing old gender stereotypes packaged into a brave new world? What is truly strange and what familiar in the digital domestic? Balfour casts a welcome critical eye upon the world coming and still to come, and on the language we have to describe it."

—Professor David Simpson, Distinguished Professor and G.B. Needham
Chair Emeritus at the *University of California Davis, USA*

Lindsay Anne Balfour

The Digital Future of Hospitality

palgrave
macmillan

Lindsay Anne Balfour 🆔
Coventry University
Coventry, UK

ISBN 978-3-031-24562-6   ISBN 978-3-031-24563-3   (eBook)
https://doi.org/10.1007/978-3-031-24563-3

This Palgrave Macmillan imprint is published by the registered company Springer Nature Switzerland AG.
The registered company address is: Gewerbestrasse 11, 6330 Cham, Switzerland

ACKNOWLEDGEMENTS

As with any project, this has been a labour of love and has been book-ended by the hospitality of friends, family, and colleagues. I am grateful especially to the Centre for Postdigital Cultures at Coventry University for generating a space of collaboration, conversation, and intellectual curiosity where the ideas here could be shared and tested.

This book is dedicated to those strangers I have yet to meet—human, digital, and more-than-human. And to those I know already and without whom this project would not be possible. To Doug and Cheryl for endless support, encouragement, and childcare. To my mother, Charlotte, whose spirit unfolds the best in all of us; I hope we can always see the world the way you did. To Scott, for dreaming with me and believing *in* me—our best is yet to come. And to my children—Aidan and Cordelia—my little fire, and my daughter of the sea; may you stay adventurous, curious, and kind. As always, there is no praise higher than yours.

CONTENTS

CHAPTER 1

Introduction: The Digital Future of Hospitality

In October 2020, right before Halloween, the dating application *Tinder* launched a new campaign designed to give users the opportunity to reconnect with an old flame they had abruptly stopped contacting. Known as "ghosting," this phenomenon has been prevalent enough in recent years to find its way into the Oxford English Dictionary, where it is described as "the action of ignoring or pretending not to know a person, *esp.* that of suddenly ceasing to respond to someone on social media, by text message [or] the action of ending a relationship or association with someone by ceasing all communication" (OED 2022). In 2016, another dating app, *Plenty of Fish*, conducted a survey of 18–33-year-olds—what they classified as "millennials"—and found that 78% of them had been ghosted at least once (Zarya 2016). Whether as a means of avoiding confrontation, disappointment with the "real life" version of an online partner, or trying to slow down a relationship that is becoming too clingy, ghosting is a reality of relationships initiated and negotiated in online space. It is also a curious terminology, one that conjures (pun intended, notions of erasure, haunting, and the return of the digital dead).

Tinder's campaign, playfully called "It's Your Boo," offers a remediation of a disturbing trend, whereby former "ghosts" (i.e. those who disappeared without warning) are given opportunity to reach out to those they left hanging months or years ago. While "ghosting" has been in social media vernacular for several years now, Tinder's timing here is particularly apt. Drawing on seasonal cues of loneliness, combined with the increased online dating activity associated with the COVID-19 pandemic, "It's Your Boo" claims "2020 is scary enough. This Halloween, Tinder is giving you the chance to unghost someone and bring that dead chat back to life" (Tinder 2022). While at first glance Tinder's new service seems like an important opportunity for users to make amends, rekindle a romance, or—at very least—apologize for past behaviour and move forward guilt-free, it also reveals the figure of the ghost—or what we might call *spectrality*—to be thoroughly enmeshed in digital life, where online space is punctuated by gaps and absences, anonymized neglect and a cultural obsession with disappearance. Digital life, in other words, is *already* haunted by promised and failed forms of intimacy with strangers and, ultimately, *Tinder's* attempts to bring such ghosts back from the dead speak to a deep preoccupation with a philosophy of hospitality and a reality of living with others, whether human or more-than-human, virtual or material, that is more critical than ever.

Spectral Hospitality

While ghosting is in part cultural vernacular, and part contemporary fascination with the supernatural, it is also a theoretical figure and just one digital reanimation of what this book explores—that is, the philosophical concept of hospitality. This book explores many different understandings of what that means, all of which navigate around the central definition of hospitality as the welcome of the stranger (Derrida 2000b). Hospitality, like the ghost, is nothing new; it has a past, a genealogy, and an etymology. It reaches back to pre-Enlightenment encounters with strangers, and traces back further still, to the Homeric,[1] Persian, Abrahamic, and Christian offers of refuge, food, and drink to guests and weary travellers who have been a part of literary and oral narratives for millennia. Hospitality reaches forward as well, in a bid to reconcile contemporary social, cultural, and political challenges through deconstructionist, ethical, political (i.e.

---

[1] Such traditions also allude to hospitality's contradictory enactment and the collapse of welcome into violence. At the end of Homer's *The Odyssey*, for instance, the scene of hospitality—structured around Odysseus' homecoming—is overturned when the conventional objects of welcome (a footstool for guests to sit, a basket of meat) are deployed as weapons against the guests. See Steve Reece's, *The Stranger's Welcome* (Ann Arbor: University of Michigan Press, 1993) for a detailed account of hospitality in ancient Greece.

cosmopolitan), and economic debates over welcoming strangers. Most recently, primary thinking on hospitality has considered migrant life and the refugee crisis (see Yegenoglu 2012; Rosello 2001; Baker 2011). While these concerns over human security have not waned, hospitality must now turn again to confront the most pressing global challenge from which no one is immune: our inevitable technological future.

The ghost, then, becomes such a crucial figure for both philosophy and digital life not because it appears as an invited guest online here, and as part of the *Tinder* narrative in particular, but rather because hospitality is based not on invitation at all but on visitation. Derrida describes this in detail in a conversation with contemporary philosophers Richard Kearney and Mark Dooley:

> For pure hospitality or a pure gift to occur, however, there must be an absolute surprise. The other, like the Messiah, must arrive whenever he or she wants. She [sic] may even not arrive...If I am unconditionally hospitable I should welcome the visitation, not the invited guest, but the visitor. I must be unprepared, or prepared to be unprepared, for the unexpected arrival of any other. Is this possible? I don't know. If, however, there is pure hospitality, or a pure gift, it should consist in this opening without horizon, without horizon of expectation, an opening to the newcomer whoever that may be. It may be terrible because the newcomer may be a good person, or may be the devil. (Derrida 1998)

Indeed, the spectre forces us to confront important questions, among them: Is the ghost (or any other digital stranger for that matter) a welcome guest, a hostile threat, or perhaps both? What if that "ghosted" partner does not want to be contacted? What if the return of that ghost opens new wounds or resurrects past trauma? While there has been much discussion on the practice of ghosting as an unfortunate but realistic bedfellow of dating online, it also reinforces the work of the spectral and its function as a social and cultural (rather than exclusively Gothic) figure that, I argue, expresses a philosophy of hospitality in new and important ways. Avery Gordon (1997), for instance, suggests that "ghostly matters are part of social life." Derrida, moreover, urges we "say yes to who or what turns up, before any determination, before any anticipation, before any identification, before an unexpected visitor, whether or not the new arrival is the citizen of another country, a human, animal, or divine creature, a *living or dead* thing, male or female," or, as it were, a ghost (2000b, my emphasis). Indeed, these online spectres expose a preoccupation with strangers and strangeness that extends far beyond the confines of the dating app and haunt our digital lives in many ways. Beyond "ghosting" might think of phenomena such as digital celebrity holograms,[2] 404 "File not found" errors, Facebook pages for the dead, and the language of the internet itself. We might recall also that "ghost" can refer to a chat entry lingering after the user has logged out and that "ghost imaging" is the process of transferring a shadow copy of a hard drive to a new device (Ince 2009). Nor can we forget the ways in which the phrase "the cloud" invokes visual imaginaries of the afterlife, often a kind of digital purgatory for discarded data.

Our experience with digital life, then, is an experience with multiple levels of hospitality at once—an invitation to share in strangers' lives (whether human, once-human, or more-than-human), but also, on a more compelling level, an unbidden haunting and an ethical imperative that emphasizes our profound relationality. In *Seeing Ghosts: 9/11 and the Visual Imagination*, Karen Engle (2009) notes, "in as much as we are, we are by virtue of others passing through our lives, memories, and bodies." Judith Butler elaborates further: "none of us is fully bounded, utterly separate but, rather, we are *in our skins, given over*, in each other's hands, at each other's mercy" (2005, my emphasis). What is this passing, or scrolling, through other lives, and other lives passing through us, and our skin, if not the very definition of ghostly possession? Hospitality is, unequivocally and even traumatically, possession of another, by another, and for another without recourse to exorcism. It is what defines (and destroys) our sociality and our relations with others. It is also, in Derrida's words, "culture itself and not simply one ethic among others…[It is] the manner in which we relate to ourselves and to others, to others as our own or as foreigners[…]ethics is so thoroughly coextensive with the experience of hospitality" (2001). If, then, hospitality is everywhere, and indistinguishable from ethics itself, it must be understood and clarified in terms of how its genealogy lands now on the doorstep of the digital.

---

[2] A popular gimmick at recent music concerts and festivals, holograms have been developed to support the stage resurrection of artists such as Frank Sinatra, Elvis, Tupac Shakur (more digital effect than hologram), Michael Jackson, and Amy Winehouse. As the technology for this improves, debates rage on about the ethics of purchasing rights to reanimate dead celebrities in holographic form; these "rights" include access not only to a music of film archive but also to the deceased's "likeness" (Tiffany 2018).

HOSPITALITY PAST AND FUTURE

We think we know what hospitality is—we have a common language to describe it and are familiar with its rituals of welcome and invitation, giving shelter or protection and, in political terms, the figures of asylum and immigration. Herein lies an important distinction between what Derrida describes as a pure or absolute hospitality, and its more political counterpart—the laws of hospitality (what Kant would call cosmopolitanism). In Derrida's words, there is a difference between

> the law of unlimited hospitality (to give the new arrival all of one's home and oneself, to give him or her one's own, our own, without asking a name, or compensation, or the fulfilment of even the smallest condition), and on the other hand, the laws (in the plural), those rights and duties that are always conditioned and conditional, as they are defined by the Greco-Roman tradition and even the Judaeo-Christian one, by all of law and all philosophy of law up to Kant and Hegel in particular, across the family, civil society, and the State. (Derrida 2000b)

Whether by its laws or the law, we have also seen hospitality fail—evidenced by closed borders, vaccine passports, and the denial of refuge to asylum seekers around the globe. Ethical or political, however, we can recognize its figures which remain constant: doors and thresholds, entrances, gates, and stoops that demarcate the familiar and foreign. These figures, we can "comprehend" because, in Jacques Derrida's words: "[T]hey belong to the current lexicon or the common semantics of hospitality, of all precomprehension of what 'hospitality' is and means, namely, to 'welcome,' 'accept,' 'invite,' 'receive,' 'bid' someone welcome 'to one's home'" (Derrida 2000b). And so, while this volume confronts a future-oriented digital archive never before considered in the context of hospitality, it is also critical to recognize the depth of hospitality's endurance over time. Contemporary Western thinking about hospitality can be traced back to Immanuel Kant and his influential Third Definitive Article in *Toward Perpetual Peace* (1795, 2003). For Kant, hospitality is a question of right and not of philanthropy—"the right of a stranger not to be treated as an enemy when he arrives in the land of another" (1795, 2003). Yet Kant's original formulation seems more attuned to the political possibility of the *laws* of hospitality rather than it absolute or pure imperative, for his hospitality is one premised on "behave[ing] peaceably" (1795, 2003). Thus, Kant's cosmopolitan right is limited to the visitor who does not yet become a guest—it is a right to *temporary* visitation and that visitor may only *request* permanent residence. Significantly, then, hospitality is not unconditional—if the would-be guest is not harmed by the denial of entry, the host is under no obligation to accept him. In Kant's words, "if it can be done without destroying him, he can be turned away" (1795, 2003). For Romantic scholar David Simpson, Kant's conditions of universal hospitality pose significant limitations to the ethics of open and absolute welcome. Kant's ethic certainly goes beyond the formalities of obligation and the meeting of basic needs; however, as Simpson (2013) claims, its particular ethical imperative requires little more than "the foundation for a commercial relationship"—perhaps the kind of relationship we will discover in this book's discussion of Uber and Airbnb. As such, it is not unconditional hospitality, as Derrida would define it. Rather, "absolute hospitality requires that I open up my home and that I give not only give to the foreigner, but to the absolute, unknown, anonymous other, and that I give place to them, that I let them come, that I let them arrive, and take place in the place I offer them, without asking of them either reciprocity (entering into a pact) or even their names" (2000a). Nonetheless, Kant remains a critical figure for thinking about how hospitality might still operate as opposed to an impossible ethic that remains elusive or always at a distance.

In many ways, however, we need not a definition from Kant, Derrida, or any philosopher; we have a shared vocabulary and sense of the laws of hospitality as they unfold (and are often neglected) in the political and juridical spheres, in cultural products, spectacles of media, and even in our visual imagination. *But what about digital life?* While the particular twenty-first-century philosophy of hospitality I offer here is certainly an inheritor of Derridean thought, the digital pushes us more than ever to consider hospitality in new ways. Derrida *was* always a thinker of the future, indeed, hospitable *to* the future, refusing to put limits or conditions on its arrival. This volume, however, draws much from continental philosophy but extends and adapts it here to consider what hospitality means in an entirely new kind of social and cultural milieu, where the digital unfolds in every aspect of our relationality with people, technologies, and ourselves. Each chapter recognizes the durability of hospitality over time, but engages new ideas and thinkers in the service of developing a theory of hospitality suitable, situated, and critical to our (post)digital times. At the same time, this book does not take the digital as ubiquitous or taken for granted, nor does it present technology as our "last or best hope" in the vein of Star Wars-esque prophecy. The contemporary philosopher Richard Kearney, for instance, *warns* us of the limits of a technologically determined future—one that may announce *and* annul intimate relations with others and what he calls a "carnal hospitality." In his words, "our current technology is arguably exacerbating our carnal alienation. While offering us enormous freedoms of fantasy and encounter, digital eros may also be removing us further from the flesh"—a flesh, he argues, that is integral to the ethic of hospitality (2014). Is the digital alienating us from relationships with others? Do we need to return, in Kearney's words (2014), "from iCloud to earth" and re-materialize lives made spectral by digital obsession? And are digital life, smartphones, platform economies, and dating apps the absence of hospitality? Or do they simply reveal the deep internal complexity of a philosophy of strangers and strangeness and actually *energize* new relations, opportunities, and intimacies? It seems that when thinking about the relationship between hospitality and digital life, these contradictions become even more apparent. Not only does hospitality deconstruct itself when put into practice, but also it is internally inconsistent, practically, and even etymologically, and that which it requires to make achievable is the same thing that renders it impossible. So too does the digital present us with alternating (and, at time, contradictory) possibilities for living with others, human or more-than-human. The figure of the door is a useful illustration of how hospitality can be updated for digital times without abandoning its ethical force or complexity. Indeed, for there to be hospitality, there must be a door that one could open to whoever is on the other side. But Derrida (2000b) reminds us, "If there is a door, there is no longer hospitality." This is the difference—"the gap"—between a "hospitality of invitation and the hospitality of visitation" (Derrida 2000b). It is also a gap we see reflected everywhere in online life and digital technologies: the closed doors or gatekeeping figures of everything from passwords and permissions to multi-factor authentication and biometric identification, spam filters, Asimov blocks,[3] VPNs, computer viruses, firewalls, and the

---

[3] Isaac Asimov's short story collection *I, Robot* (1968) imagined the relationship between humans and machines, long before the technology ever existed to make that relationship possible. In this series, he asks readers to imagine a world where robots protect us from our own worst nature and reveals an overarching vision of a future that entangles inextricably the humans and the machines. According to Asimov, anyone clever enough to create robots would also be smart enough to make sure that those robots would not attack their makers. Conceived by Asimov as the Three Laws of Robotics—essential laws built into the robots' inner workings—these protections of "Asimov blocks" freed science fiction writers to develop robots as characters instead of portraying them as monstrous things. See Chap. 2 of this volume for an extended discussion of how Asimov's Laws are portrayed on television.

literal screens that separate human from hardware. The digital, clearly, has its own doors to alternately welcome or ward off uninvited strangers.

Hospitality and Digital Life

How then, to work through a philosophy of welcome in a world where the digital future is very much a source of both anxiety and promise, and in a social age where we are, due in part to the role of the device itself, in Kearney's (2014) words, "losing our touch"? How is digital culture changing hospitality, and could the reverse also be true? We have all been guests and hosts, with a myriad of results and expectations. The rhetoric of invitation and reception, the gifting of food and drink, and the opening of doors to one's home or nation—these are the images of hospitality enshrined predominantly in a rhetoric of etiquette and entertainment. Entire industries, and even economic empires, have been built on the premise of welcoming guests and, while this study is not about the hospitality industry *per se*, that is not to say that the provisions of safe passage, shelter, and food are not crucial ports through which a philosophical or ethical hospitality is both lived and often disavowed, as well as a familiar point of reference. Even, however, as these more commercial rituals are bound in relations of exchange, reciprocity, and (often conspicuous) consumption, surely they still provide a framework by which we can identify ethical relations between hosts and guests. Why then does Derrida (2000b) insist (emphatically and at length) "we do not know what hospitality is"? Could it be he is referencing an event of hospitality that we have yet to (and may not ever) see? Or perhaps Derrida's hospitality "to come" is, in fact, his prophecy of the present we now inhabit. Perhaps hospitality "to come" is now here, in the emergence of the digital—a spectre of virtual welcome and, alternately, hostility that has now, there can be no doubt, *arrived*. Indeed, hospitality is ubiquitous but also historical, and there is something unique to *this* moment—an era of social networking, virtual domestic assistants, artificial consciousness, the under-questioned ubiquity of the "web*host*" and "*home*page," the body-machine assemblage, and our obsession (stronger than ever) with viruses and immunity, on and off our screens. It cannot be denied, hospitality is both critically needed and more difficult than ever. Is it here then, in the anticipation of this digital future, where we find the limits of hospitality tested? Is this where hospitality runs out? Or is this where it might begin?

In *Hospitality in a Time of Terror: Strangers at the Gate* (Balfour 2017), I argued that the encounter with strangers was at the core of cultural production and culture itself in the aftermath of the terrorist attacks of 11 September 2001. I documented the significance of hospitality after 9/11, particularly as such an ethic is so provocatively raised or disavowed by a predominantly visual and cultural archive that has been and continues to be consumed by millions of people around the world. This book utilized works of cultural memory, film, art, and literature that show the breadth of hospitality's influence but that offer a depth of insight, historical specificity, and theoretical intensity that only a product created in the aftermath of 9/11 allows.

Again, and in ways similar to the preoccupation with strangers that arose after 9/11, hospitality is, once again, "in crisis and at a crossroad" (Balfour 2017) and is more relevant than ever in a digital age that is only intensifying and where a discourse of unconditional welcome is made possible but also challenged by the particular conditions of social and cultural life that emerge through technology. But if hospitality is an ethic of welcome, it is also one of violence. Simpson, for example, reminds us of the translations of the root words *xenos* (Greek) and *hôte* (French), which designate "either host or guest or both at once, so that those who appear to differ—one at home and the other coming to the house and requesting hospitality—are bound together etymologically as codependent and perhaps even interchangeable: every host is a guest in the making, every stranger is familiar" (Simpson 2013). Hospitality, as this etymology shows us, is constantly invaded by the thing it supposedly opposes—that is, hostility—and presents a challenge in terms of how we might think through a word that seems to cancel its own purpose. Hospitality, thus, while conjuring a particular set of images, has always been an unstable concept. It is here that the digital perhaps exposes the limits of philosophy, as news headlines, popular entertainment, and social media recall the countless stories of those who have suffered *actual* violence as a result of the virtual world. From cyberbullying and harassment to revenge porn, social exclusion, internet dating scams, ghosting, and technologically driven assaults and disappearances, the digital is anything *but* hospitable for many.

Digital life, then, reminds us that hospitality, in its absolute sense, never promises safety from harm, and the purest expression of hospitality may, in fact, lead to death—a figure that even Kant paradoxically invokes when he begins his treatise on cosmopolitanism by musing on a Dutch Innkeeper's sign.[4] This sign contains the image of a graveyard at the same time as it advertises "Perpetual Peace" (Kant, 1795, 2003). Indeed, if absolute hospitality is an openness to whoever or whatever arrives, then included in that is a hospitality even to the one who brings the perpetual peace that only comes from the endless sleep of death. In other words, the one who comes to kill—perhaps now represented by the android, the machine replacement, or the computer virus. The prospect reminds us that hospitality has never been about invitation—seeking out the guests who come only to do good. On the contrary, it is about a hospitality to those or that which may arrive precisely to do us harm or, more chillingly, may come disguised as a welcome guest and wreak destruction once arrived.

It is particularly telling that the internet is already preoccupied with a discourse of hospitality, in its very linguistic structure. "Home" page and web "host" have been used ubiquitously for years with little consideration of what this language entails for the practice of hospitality and the fascination with discourses of guests and hosts. The technology of the home page is, for all intents and purposes, a gatekeeper; a bastion of potential *inhospitable* welcome, designed to interface potential "outsiders"—manifesting here in the form of disruptive notifications, left-field friend requests from total strangers, and intruding reminders to update one's software. As Lucas Intona and Martin Brigham (2008) suggest, "[i]n, and between, virtual communities, the boundary between the inside and the outside is always at stake, continually disrupted as virtual strangers continue to 'pop up' on our screens." We might think, then, of the homepage as a virtual threshold, where relations between self and other are tested, and where the line between private and shared space is complicated, precarious, and password protected.

That these hosting mechanisms are now carried around with us at all times—in the form of mobile devices—disrupts the notion of a physical threshold, the spatiality of hospitable welcome, and the stability of a host who is now *not* at home and who cannot even accept a guest at all, invited or not. Far from being the absence of hospitality, however, perhaps this is the pinnacle. Is the stranger not meant to disturb the being-at-home with oneself? And does that arrival, in the words of Emmanuel Levinas (1969), not imply "the interruption of a full possession of a place called home"? And so, even thinking through the possibility of a web "host" designates

[4] I will return to Kant and his concept of cosmopolitanism as a baseline for Uber and Airbnb's promotion of "global citizenship" within the platform economy in Chap. 4.

a tenuous position between hospitality and hostility, and the role of a host who is, for all intents and purposes, displaced vis-à-vis their mobility. This is, of course, not to overwrite the real lived experience of those displaced through war, ecological disaster and uncertainty, food shortage, or persecution. Nowhere are both the material and ethical questions of hosts and guests more acute than in the plight of millions of people around the world forced to flee their homes. Even here, however, hospitality and digital life are deeply entangled. Writing on the use of mobile technology by migrants—those who are, essentially, "home" less, Gillian Whitlock (2015) finds promise in the spaces afforded by mobile technology, suggesting that these are thresholds "where the boundaries between self and other, citizen and stranger, are constantly under negotiation. This intersection occurs in physical and virtual spaces, and in technologies of the self that are transformed in the performative new spaces enabled by Web 2.0 technologies." Cyberspace here offers a hospitality where physical space has failed, a landing site at which to be welcomed rather than a border where one is turned away. As Whitlock (2015) describes "those consigned to the 'socially dead'—asylum seekers, indentured labour, and detainees[5]—now travel with mobile digital devices that capture evidence of abjection and captivity with unprecedented intimacy, and disseminate their testimonial narratives to a global networked public." Each landing site then, whether a webpage or a beach shoring up migrant boats, acts as this threshold of both risk and possibility. Thinking about the homepage as a complicated site of landing not only reminds us of the precarity of arrival for displaced guests around the globe, but also exposes how the conditions of welcome are often archived in technologically mediated ways, as the digital becomes not only a site or location of arrival, but also a testimonial tool and a narrative witness to the interactions of guests and hosts.

In what follows, I work through both the failures and promises of hospitality via a series of digital cultural texts, almost all of which have immediate relevance to our daily lives. Beyond Web 2.0, social media, and Apple watches, the digital is changing the way we engage with others and

---

[5] Whitlock's description of the "socially dead" here returns productively to the notion of spectral hospitality and the ghost as the stranger *par excellence*. At the same time, the notion of detainees recalls not only the socio-political experience of abjection/rejection, but also the very real practice of black site prisons and extraordinary rendition where so-called ghost detainees are spirited away via clandestine and extra-juridical methods (see Pugliese 2013).

strangers as hospitality has become more "mobile" than ever. But if this is an exploration of the future, it is also a casting backwards; indeed, technology has *always* haunted us with its indeterminable prospects. At the same time, we are dealing not only with these enduring philosophical questions, but also with the pressing socio-cultural ones that all become mediated and media*tized* through digital culture: questions around resource depletion and land access, health care, human migration and asylum, techno-anxiety and digital access, surveillance, globalization, terrorism, food sovereignty, market volatility, indigeneity, and human rights. Our hopes and our fear are always, Derrida reminds us, about what is "to come." Yet these hopes and fears now transcend the solely material and intersect in an unprecedented proliferation of 1s and 0s, where even our most complex social, cultural, and political challenges are being taken up by tech CEOs and software engineers. Indeed, as Apple declared, and trademarked in 2009, only three years after the word "Google" entered the OED, whatever your challenge may be, "*there's an app for that*" (Brownlee 2010).

Specifically, this book tests the future of hospitality over the uneven terrain of new technology and digital life: the gatekeeping hostilities of the "homepage"; the android host body in popular culture; the gendered hospitality of the digital domestic—whom we refer to by names like Siri and Alexa; Uber and Airbnb—hospitality apps for the gig economy; the digital intimacies of wearable tech; and the threat of malware and cultural preoccupations with immunity. Each chapter here makes a case for both the enduring legacy and the reanimation of hospitality while reading its tensions and contradictions through the most pressing and precedent artefacts of our digital lives.

Chapter 2, "Surrogates, Androids and the Digital 'Host' Body," draws attention to the recent proliferation of popular television that leverages the digital in the service of both promising and problematic forms of hospitality, and the emergence of the android "host" as a pervasive television figure. While the android has been a visual marker of science fiction books, film, and television for decades, it has shifted somewhat to question the integrity of digital users, and the extent to which technology is or should be controlling our lives. In other words, far from being a symbol of threat and invasion, the android now is often used as a foil to unethical and violent *human* behaviour. In short, these androids reveal far more about us—our relationship to technology, our role as both hosts and guests, and our capacity for violence—than they do about their own dangerous intentions, particularly as such figures are now regularly deployed in real life scenarios that span sex to war. We are prompted, then, to ask how television and other forms of contemporary popular culture both contain and exacerbate concerns about the future of artificial consciousness and the sentience of the "host" body as such figures move not just into proximity but into relationality, with humans. Made over in our image, these android hosts both provide a familiarization of our technological fear *and* fulfil our deepest desires of living forever. Here, we are forced to consider not only if the android can feel but also if hospitality itself is only a *human* ethic. Indeed, if violence continues to be woven into the very core of humanity's new surrogates, what do they then tell us about humanity itself?

Chapter 3—"Violence, Gendered Labour, and the Hospitality of the Digital Domestic"—extends thinking about the embodied android figure towards virtual assistants such as Siri and Alexa, who are without human form and therefore exercise their hospitality in the absence of corporeality or touch. In this way we might think of virtual assistants as representative of what Intona and Brigham (2008) call the "thinness of the virtual" rather than the "thickness of the flesh." While not writing on Siri and Alexa, their questions are remarkably significant when thinking through the hospitality of the digital domestic. "Can I encounter the other as Other in virtuality?" they ask, invoking the Levinasian figure of the face as a condition for ethical encounter (Intona and Brigham 2008). Do Siri and Alexa have a face—that singular figure for absolute alterity which demands our ethical response? Siri and Alexa may not be coded as human, but they *are* coded as feminine, act out in anthropomorphic ways, and raise serious questions about how hospitality is leveraged through both gendered intimacy and gendered labour.

This chapter ultimately suggests that artificially intelligent virtual assistants do not create new relations of power and violence but rather reflect those of old—specifically latent and *Orientalist* notions of gender difference and sexual violence now conveniently repackaged in digital form. Drawing on critical theories of race, (post)feminism, and surveillance capitalism, I bring attention to an underexplored form of sexual violence—that is projected onto virtual assistants—and consider how the gendered hospitality of the digital domestic reminds us of historical animations of gender and excess, privacy and intimacy, and the Orientalist fantasies of the Ottoman harem. At first glance, the harem does not seem to have much to do with these contemporary cultural texts, yet it actually provides a convincing metaphor for thinking about hospitality's crucial relation to the discourses of intimacy, labour, and surveillance that operate in voice-activated domestic assistants. It is also an apt methodological figure—an imaginative conjuring—that underwrites and even haunts the representation of gender and violence within technology.

Chapter 4 offers an analysis of digital labour and the sheer volume of mobile apps dedicated to the selling and exchanging of hospitality services. "Sharing Spaces: Stranger Encounters the Gig Economy" traces the most notable and successful of these—Airbnb and Uber—which facilitate a kind of hosting that is commodified, to be sure, but interestingly mediated through the private space of one's home or vehicle. These networks, both social and transactional, present significant opportunity for thinking through the role of hosts and guests in on- *and* offline space.

What makes Airbnb and Uber, with their model of pre-emptive annulment, such an abdication of hospitality is the evacuation of ethical alterity from any level of encounter. Hospitality is thus datafied and ultimately forestalled by the conditional algorithms already in place before the meeting can ever occur. Yet the premise of both platforms remains remarkably attuned to the project of hospitality and reminds us of both the instability, but also the potential intimacy, of relations between strangers. Here, hospitality is not so much a matter of human-computer interaction but of digitally facilitated *human-human* interaction. Yet these apps also prompt us to think about the forms of intimacy generated by technology *beyond* kinship and the hetero-relationality of dating apps. Hospitality is a strange intimacy whereby—in the context of gig economy apps—the digital is inextricable from the relations we have, and the world we inhabit. Drawing again on feminist intersectionality, as well as theorists of urban geography and affect, this chapter considers the spatiality of digital encounters between strangers, simultaneously distant but at the same time more embodied than ever, and part of a complex network of relations between humans, computers, and the environments that sustain both. In the context of hospitality, Uber and Airbnb are anything but straightforward; instead, they inform and animate particular spaces of intimacy as contradictory and complex and challenge some of hospitality's enduring dualisms of inside(r)/outside(r), public and private, human and non-human (or more-than-human) and embodied and not.

Finally, Chap. 5, "Digital Intimacy in Biometric Technologies," considers the intimate forms of hospitality exposed through the proliferation of wearable, implantable, or ingestible technologies. Specifically, I explore how the kinds of touch involved in biometric devices operate on the threshold of the foreign and familiar, occupying what robotics professor

Masahiro Mori (1970) calls the "uncanny valley." Thinking about the extent to which digital replicas and prostheses offer alternating affects of comfort or uncertainty raises a number of serious questions for theories of strangeness so crucial to hospitality, as our own bodies, through data, are made strangers to us. As such, this chapter maps the psychoanalysis of Kristeva, Freud, and others, onto a theory of hospitality as an entanglement of self-(ac)knowledge(ment) and self-estrangement.

This chapter explores forms of embodied computing including wearables (Fitbit, the Apple Watch, among others), as well as the larger spectrum of products we refer to as "FemTech."[6] Gendered biometric technologies produce a knowledge of the Quantified Self[7] that is equal parts reassuring and alarming, using the familiarity and comfort of the body itself, hosting our biometric data and guiding us through its interpretation while at the same time assuaging fears about the digital unknown. Through these devices, we are turned inside out, and that which we used to call familiar and homely—food and drink, sleep, speech and heart rate, and more—is no longer ours. It is external to us (*even if implanted within our own bodies*), datafied, and governed. It doesn't just reveal our desires; it gives us new ones by way of targeted step counts and recommended calorie intake, tells us when (and when not) to have sex, and uncovers what's beneath the surface of our skin through an intimate diagnostic process.

This chapter then asks, in part, how is it that touch, as a sense (and, in this case, *sensor*), can be both comfortable, familiar, and *homely*, while at the same time unfamiliar, strange, unsettling, and uncanny? Moreover, how might we read the excarnation of digital technology as a kind of estrangement, but one brought back to the body as an unfamiliar datametrics, making us—in Kristeva's words—strangers to ourselves? How does the body itself act as a border between flesh and code, the tactile and

---

[6] "FemTech" refers to the rapidly evolving market of digital health products and interventions (including both software and hardware) marketed to women, including ovulation, pregnancy and fitness trackers, reproductive technologies, apps for sexual wellness, menopause, and health challenges such as endometriosis and PCOS, contraceptive microchips and "smart" pills, and more.

[7] Quantified self refers both to the cultural phenomenon of self-tracking with technology and to a community of users and makers of self-tracking tools who share an interest in self-knowledge through numbers. Quantified self-practices overlap with other trends that incorporate technology and data acquisition into daily life, often with the goal of improving physical, mental, and/or emotional performances.

the digital, and how is this breached in the case of wearable or ingestible technology? At its core, this analysis suggests that, much like George Grinnell's (2020) reading of border surveillance, there is a "social life" of biometrics that reminds us of the ways in which hospitality is leveraged according to differential regimes of readability and recognition, not the least of which is how we read ourselves.

HOSPITALITY FOR A DIGITAL FUTURE

Whether in the form of the synthetic android host, the machine-learning digital assistant, the commodified intimacy of the guest-host relationship in home and ride-sharing apps, or the foreign and familiar invasions of biometric technology, hospitality has become data. Established philosophies of hospitality tell us that pure and unconditional welcome is impossible because we will always apprehend the other within our own routines of subjective identification. But perhaps data is then the ultimate stranger, an absolute other that never subsumes into *self*. More importantly, if the forms of digital hospitality explored here tell us anything, it is that the data controls *us*—not the other way around. We are, as it turns out, *hostaged* to these lines of code. Indeed, hospitality, at times, seems to cancel its own purpose with its "troubled and troubling origin"; it is "a word which carries its own contradiction incorporated into it, a Latin word which allows itself to be parasitized by its opposite, 'hostility,' the undesirable guest [hôte] which it harbors as the self-contradiction in its own body" (Derrida 2000b).

My purpose, therefore, is to read the digital as an alternating figure of failed and *potential* hospitality, which is everywhere in digital culture, yet tremendously underexplored. Undoubtedly, thinking about digital life through the concept of hospitality offers a new avenue for exploring the implications of virtual technologies on our ethical, social, and cultural life, as well as providing a new way to think about the problem of hospitality itself. As Derrida declares, "[h]ospitality must be so inventive, adjusted to the other, and to the welcoming of the other, that each experience of hospitality must invent a new language" (in Brown 2010). So, too, must we be inventive in our own apprehension of the concept? David Simpson's (2006) question on the genealogy of mourning is also particularly useful here, as he asks, "Has there ever been a time that was not the time of death?" Indeed, has there ever been a time that was not the time of hospitality? Or a time that was not a time of technology? These digital texts do not offer a blueprint to find a pure and unconditional welcome; but if there was ever a time to revisit such an ethic in earnest, it is now, in this era of increasing mobility, apps for everything, social media, artificial intelligence, and the collapse of the human-machine binary. What I offer here is therefore ultimately future-oriented, anticipating further discussion over the anthropomorphism of virtual and digital life, the extent to which humans themselves are coded (by history, culture, and more), and in the service of a *prospect* of human-computer interaction where hospitality is determined not on the basis of a human ontological subject but on reciprocal ethics of alterity and co-dependence.

REFERENCES

Airbnb.com. 2022. *Airbnb Inc.*
Asimov, Isaac. 1968. *I, Robot.* Harper Collins.
Atanasoski, Neda, and Kalindi Vora. 2019. *Surrogate Humanity: Race, Robots and the Politics of Technological Futures.* Duke University Press.
Baker, Gideon. 2011. *Politicising Ethics in International Relations: Cosmopolitanism and Hospitality.* Routledge.
Balfour, Lindsay. 2017. *Hospitality in a Time of Terror: Strangers at the Gate.* Rowman & Littlefield.
Bloechl, Jeffrey. 2011. Words of Welcome: Hospitality in the Philosophy of Emmanuel Levinas. In *Phenomenologies of the Stranger: Between Hostility and Hospitality*, ed. Richard Kearney and Kascha Semonovitch. Fordham University Press.
Booker, Charlie. 2011. *Black Mirror.* Channel 4/Netflix.
Borradori, Giovanna. 2003. *Philosophy in a Time of Terror: Dialogues with Jürgen Habermas and Jacques Derrida.* University of Chicago Press.
Braidotti, Rosi. 2013. *The Posthuman.* Cambridge: Polity.
———. 2015. Posthuman Affirmative Biopolitics. In *Resisting Biopolitics: Philosophical, Political, and Performative Strategies*, ed. S.E. Wilmer and Audroné Žukauskaité. New York: Routledge.
Brown, Garrett W. 2010. The Laws of Hospitality, Asylum Seekers and Cosmopolitan Right: A Kantian Response to Jacques Derrida. *European Journal of Political Theory* 9. https://doi.org/10.1177/1474885110363983.
Brownlee, John. 2010. Apple Gets a Trademark: There's an App for That. *Cult of Mac.* https://www.cultofmac.com/62892/apple-gets-a-trademark-theres-an-app-for-that/.
Butler, Judith. 2005. *Giving and Account of Oneself.* Fordham University Press.
Burke, Edmond. 2005. *The Works of the Right Honorable Edmund Burke.* Project Gutenberg EBook. Vol. I. (of 12). https://www.gutenberg.org/files/15043/15043-h/15043-h.htm.

Derrida, Jacques. 1998. Hospitality, Justice and Responsibility: A Dialogue with Jacques Derrida. In *Questioning Ethics: Contemporary Debates in Philosophy*, ed. Richard Kearney and Mark Dooley. Routledge.

———. 1999. *Adieu to Emmanuel Levinas*. Translated by Pascale-Anne Brault and Michael Naas. Stanford University Press.

———. 2000a. Hospitality. *Angelaki: Journal of the Theoretical. Humanities* 5 (3). https://doi.org/10.1080/09697250020034706.

———. 2000b. *Of Hospitality: Anne Dufourmantelle Invites Jacques Derrida to Respond*. Stanford University Press.

———. 2001. *On Cosmopolitanism and Forgiveness*. Routledge.

———. 2005a. *Rogues, Two Essays on Reason*. Translated by Pascale-Anne Brault and Michael Naas. Stanford University Press.

———. 2005b. The Principle of Hospitality. *Parallax* 11 (1). https://doi.org/1 0.1080/1353464052000321056.

Descartes, René. 1993 (1641). *Meditations on First Philosophy*. Translated by Donald A. Cress. Hackett.

Engle, Karen. 2009. *Seeing Ghosts: 9/11 and the Visual Imagination*. McGill University Press.

Esposito, Robert. 2008. *Bios: Biopolitics and Philosophy*. Minneapolis, MN: University of Minnesota Press.

Freud, Sigmund. 2003. *The Uncanny*. Translated by David McClintock. Penguin Books.

Ghosting. 2022. *Oxford English Dictionary Online*. https://www.oed.com/

Gordon, Avery. 1997. *Ghostly Matters: Haunting and the Sociological Imagination*. University of Minnesota Press.

Grinnell, George C. 2020. *The Social Life of Biometrics*. Rutgers University Press.

Haraway, Donna. 2003. *The Companion Species Manifesto: Dogs, People, and Significant Otherness*. Prickly Paradigm Press.

———. 2016. *A Cyborg Manifesto: Science, Technology and Socialist-Feminism in the Late Twentieth Century*. University of Minnesota Press.

Ince, Darrel, ed. 2009. Ghost. In *Dictionary of the Internet*. Oxford University Press.

Intona, Lucas and Martin Brigham. 2008. Derrida, Business, Ethics. In *Conference Proceedings, Centre for Philosophy and Political Economy*. University of Leicester.

Kant, Immanuel. 1915 (1795). *Perpetual Peace, a Philosophical Essay*. Translated by M. Campbell Smith. London, G. Allen & Unwin ltd.

Kearney, Richard. 2014. Losing our Touch. *New York Times*. https://opinionator. blogs.nytimes.com/2014/08/30/losing-our-touch.

———. 2019. Double Hospitality Between Word and Touch. *Journal for Continental Philosophy of Religion* 1. https://doi.org/10.1163/258896 13-00101005.

Kearney, Richard, and Brian Treanor. 2015. Introduction Carnal Hermeneutics from Head to Foot. In *Carnal Hermeneutics*. Fordham: New York.

Levinas, Emmanuel. 1969. *Totality and Infinity*. Translated by Alphonso Lingis. Duquesne University Press.

Lupton, Deborah. 2016. *The Quantified Self*. Wiley.

Mitchell, W.J.T. 2005. Picturing Terror: Derrida's Autoimmunity. *Cardozo Law Review* 27 (2). https://doi.org/10.1086/511494.

Mitchell, Peta. 2017. Contagion, Virology, Autoimmunity: Derrida's Rhetoric of Contamination. *Parallax* 23 (1): 77–93.

Mori, Masahiro. 2012 (1970). The Uncanny Valley. *IEEE Robotics and Automation Magazine*. Translated by Karl F. MacDorman and Norri Kageki. https://ieeexplore.ieee.org/stamp/stamp.jsp?arnumber=6213238.

Nolan, Jonathan, and Lisa Joy. 2016. *Westworld*. HBO.

Pugliese, Joseph. 2013. *State Violence and the Execution of Law*. Routledge.

Redfield, Marc. 2009. *The Rhetoric of Terror: Reflections on 9/11 and the War on Terror*. New York: Fordham University Press.

Rosello, Miriam. 2001. *Postcolonial Hospitality: The Immigrant as Guest*. Stanford University Press.

Simpson, David. 2006. *9/11: The Culture of Commemoration*. University of Chicago Press.

———. 2013. *Romanticism and the Question of the Stranger*. University of Chicago Press.

Tiffany, Kaitlyn. 2018. Period-tracking Apps are Not for Women. *Vox.com*. https://www.vox.com/the-goods/2018/11/13/18079458/menstrual-tracking-surveillance-glow-clue-apple-health.

Tinder. 2022. Its Your Boo. Available at: https://www.itsyourboo.com/.

Uber.com. 2022. *Uber Technologies Inc.*

Whitlock, Gillian. 2015. The Hospitality of Cyberspace: Mobilizing Asylum Seeker Testimony Online. *Biography* 38 (2): 245–266.

Yegenoglu, Meyda. 2012. *Islam, Migrancy, and Hospitality in Europe*. Palgrave.

Zarya, Valentina. 2016. About 80% of Millennial Singles Have Been Victims of 'Ghosting.' *Fortune.com*. Available at: https://fortune.com/2016/03/28/millennial-singles-ghosting/.

CHAPTER 2

Surrogates, Androids, and the Digital Host Body

In Episode 1 of HBO's *Westworld* ("The Original," 2016), the question of guests and hosts is immediately introduced, and turns violent almost as quickly when Dolores Abernathy, Westworld's original android host, encounters the human guest known only as the "Man in Black." While this man has met Dolores many times, for her every encounter is a new one—the memories of past meetings are erased with every update of her programming. As a long-standing guest at the park, the Man in Black acts out a series of cruel fantasies, first killing both Dolores' father and her lover, before dragging her by her hair into the barn, presumably to be raped. The viewer very quickly understands that he has done this before and immediately learns that the park's hosts are not just here to provide a warm welcome and hospitality to its guests. Instead, they are a mechanism for the very worst in human behaviour to be exercised. In this episode, however, the Man in Black is not completely satisfied, even in spite of the programming of Dolores and other hosts that allow him violent acts without consequence. The Man in Black wants his experience to be even more authentic. In particular, he wants Dolores to "fight back" and wants her to *feel* pain. In his words: "When you're suffering, that is when you are most real" ("Chestnut"). In *Westworld* human "guests" can interact with android "hosts" in ways that are, at best, inconsequential in the real world and, at worst (and more common), grotesquely violent. The human visitors to the Western-themed park can abuse, assault, mock, and even kill the human-looking android cast until, of course, the very nature of *human*

L. A. Balfour, *The Digital Future of Hospitality*, https://doi.org/10.1007/978-3-031-24563-3_2

sentience is questioned. When the human guests ask the obvious question—what happens if they turn against us?—viewers come to understand that the hosts' welcome of human visitors is scripted by code and engineered in a lab, raising questions not only around whether or not the hosts can feel and think for themselves but also around whether hospitality itself is only a *human* ethic.

While the Man in Black's actions are perverse, his words offer an interesting perspective on the question of how an authentic guest experience is achieved, specifically when the other side of the relation is not human. Rather than justify his actions on the basis of sentience—in the sense that the android hosts have none—it is a form of sentience here that is highlighted as an *enhancement* of the park's version of hospitality, particularly as it is developed through suffering. In other words, the authenticity of Westworld comes through the ability of the hosts to act as if they have emotions and sensory capacity, insofar as the guests can suspend disbelief enough to participate as if the hosts are truly human and as if they are really in the Wild West. In this case, suffering fulfils one possible condition of sentience, yet it is engineered more for the enjoyment of the park's guests, than the agency of its hosts. Suffering here also reinforces one of the show's central themes—that of androids becoming more human, while the guests lose that very humanity in themselves. Unsurprisingly, the debate over what makes a human has been at the forefront of debates surrounding the show and, indeed, debates that echo through much of Western philosophy. As Nietzsche wrote in *Beyond Good and Evil*, "the discipline of suffering, of great suffering—do you not know that only this discipline has created all enhancements of man so far?" (2009), suggesting that suffering is not only a condition for being; it is also a means to human advancement. This possibility of hosts becoming-human or "enhancing" their "humanity" is reflected by Dr Ford, Westworld's founder and park director. In the finale of the first season, Dr Ford discovers that the very thing the hosts were programmed for (to provide a non-human outlet for human desire) has actually produced a more (than) human subject. Suffering, he muses, was "the thing that led the hosts to their awakening" ("The Bicameral Mind," 2016). And so hosts can shoot guns, they can fight back, and they can resist, but all within the narrative of excessive pleasure—as real as possible—that the park seeks to create for its human guests. In this same first episode, Bernard Lowe—head of Westworld's programming division—questions Dolores as he examines her:

Bernard: What if I told you … that there are no chance encounters? That you and everyone that you know were built to gratify the desires of the people that visit your world, the people that you call the newcomers? Would the things I told you change the way you think about the newcomers Dolores?

Dolores: No, of course not. We all love the newcomers. ("The Original," 2016)

It seems, at least at this point in the series, that Dolores' performance of hospitality is truly unconditional, this "yes to who or what turns up" (Derrida 2000b). Knowing, the true nature of the guest, in this case, does not change her imperative towards welcoming. She continues to host with full knowledge of potential harm and even death, but does so for the most part because she is programmed to continue her host role even in the face of bad guests. The implications here are clear; rather than suggest the guests are acting out transgressive desires in a "safe" space, *Westworld* turns a lens towards the unethical behaviour of humans by writing the capacity for consent and resistance into the host's code. Thus, while off-screen debates have often centred on the permissibility of violence against androids because they cannot feel, In *Westworld*, they *must* feel, particularly for the Man in Black whose goal in the park is to act out a fantasy of murder and non-consensual sex. In order to have this fantasy realized, Delores must have enough agency (whether programmed or not) to refuse consent, and for the Man in Black, "fighting back" is part of the appeal.

Asimov's Laws and Human-Android Relation

I begin with this scene of violence not to simply reiterate debates over the gendered and sexualized trauma within *Westworld*, or to repeat arguments for the degree to which the hosts experience sentience (however defined). Instead, I begin with this violence to recognize the unique way in which *Westworld* deploys hospitality as an unconditional ethic *at the same time* as it weaponizes hospitality against the android body. Moreover, beyond capacities for suffering and sentience, the relationship between guests and hosts is revealed to be both intimate and complex and even inverted throughout the series. Indeed, these first scenes seem to set the show up as an exploration of philosophy and ethics, more than sci-fi fantasy. It is through these intimate moments, though they may be violent, that *Westworld* exposes the bedrock of hospitality, even if philosophical hospitality itself is curiously never mentioned. Indeed, as the layers of synthetic flesh are peeled back on the android figures who come into the workshop for repair, we realize that what is perhaps the truest expression of hospitality—one borne by the hosts and offered even in the face of death—was really only part of the most recent software update. Yet, as relations in the park disintegrate, and flickers of consciousness emerge, the hosts do begin to feel pain, to question their own existence and, at a certain point, begin to *remember* their past narratives, even as they are sewn back up and sent back out into the game[1] to perform their host role over and over again.

The relationship between machines and humans has been imagined across time and disciplines and, in many ways, these philosophical and social debates over androids or robots long pre-date the hardware, technologies, and screen cultures that make them possible. Indeed, it was in the mid-twentieth century when writer and biochemistry professor Isaac

[1] There is not enough space here to sufficiently unpack the "game-play" of Westworld and, indeed, other television series that represent android hosts as pawns in a game meant for humans. Yet, it is worth briefly mentioning how hospitality becomes gamified in such contexts, where an ethic of welcome is offered as part of a system of rewards, stages of play, or competitive scenarios. Whether as video-game-style adversaries or as part of a role-play strategy, these android figures are intended to populate and build out a human playground. Digitalization, of course, has allowed many aspects of even the traditional hospitality industry to be gamified. From loyalty apps, to membership tiers, to time-sensitive challenges, we are all familiar with the myriad of ways in which food, drink, and entertainment have turned an ethical imperative—that of hosting and being hosted—into a system of competitive amusement. Absolute hospitality is thus annulled via an economic exchange and point structure whereby "guests" can progress, albeit slowly, but never lose. This all makes sense in the context of a digital games industry where the guest/host relationship is not only more clearly defined, but also consensual. Indeed, there is general agreement via terms and conditions or similar processes that surround consumer participation in loyalty programmes or game-like challenges. In other words, this is *voluntary* play, the nature and implications of which change in the context of a game where at least half of the players do not know they are playing a game, or are programmed to believe it is not a game at all. Like antagonists in a traditional video game, be it *Space Invaders* or *Kong*, these digital foes act and believe as though they are their programming. So too, do the representations of androids on television mimic a video game aesthetic, some shows even crossing over into video game and even board game territory as is the case in *Altered Carbon*, a table-top role-playing game (RPG) based on the Netflix programme of the same name. There is no doubt that the relationships between humans and androids, as well as the storylines, tend to mimic that of games. This includes survival and horror games (see television shows such as *American Horror Story: Apocalypse* or *Raised by Wolves*), fashion or "dress up" games (*My Living Doll*), RPG (*Westworld*), and simulation games (several episodes of *Black Mirror*).

Asimov introduced the concept of human-robot relations to our literary consciousness, in part to address anxieties over whether or not robots are here to harm or to help. His *I, Robot* (1950) series imagines a future where humans and robots might coexist, and develops what Asimov terms the "Three Laws of Robotics" in anticipation of human concerns around the future of technology. Importantly, Asimov's laws are intended to assuage such fears about a robot species dominating humans rather than contribute to technophobic anxiety. The laws, briefly, state:

1. a robot may not injure a human being or, through inaction, allow a human being to come to harm;
2. a robot must obey the orders given it by human beings except where such orders would conflict with the First Law;
3. a robot must protect its own existence as long as such protection does not conflict with the First or Second Law. (Asimov, "Runaround," 1942, 1950)

Asimov's laws act not only as a justification for humans' acceptance of automated beings; they also bring the legacies of robotics and hospitality into conversation. In many ways, they are not unlike the laws governing the programming of *Westworld*'s hosts, particularly the Third Law, which gives a robot enough agency to protect itself, but also guarantees a human victory. Indeed, this is the very reason Dolores' scripted romantic interest, Teddy, is unable to fight back against the Man in Black's violence. In *Westworld*, hosts weapons do not carry real bullets, cannot seriously harm a human, and fail completely if directed at a guest's head. These mechanisms are coded to keep the robotics program of the park aligned with Asimov's laws, yet are sidestepped slightly in inscribing the hosts with the capacity to develop relationship with the guests of their own accord. Still, their script will not allow for harm to come to a human, begging the question of how and to what extent such code can be overridden, either through new programming or perhaps through an emerging consciousness. Indeed, in Episode 6 of Season 1 ("The Adversary," 2016), the host Maeve intentionally allows herself to be killed in the park so she can be sent to the lab. When she wakes up, she convinces the technicians to allow her access to her own programming, where she confidently turns up her own "intelligence" level to its maximum potential. Not only do Maeve's actions reveal the limits of so-called Asimov Blocks, they also suggest that code itself is not a permanent script for the hosts of *Westworld* and can be easily manipulated, even by the hosts themselves.

Thinking, then, about these relations (what is often termed HCI, or human-computer interaction) through the context of hospitality adds a new dimension to debates over the sentience of future androids, the acceleration of such relationships, and the ethical responsibilities to non-human others, not to mention a reflection on the laws of hospitality themselves. It would be tempting to argue that *Westworld* embodies the very definition of the Law of hospitality, in that the hosts perform their welcoming role even when death is imminent. Writing on Derridean hospitality, Mark Westmoreland explains, "in order to be hospitable, the host must rid himself of security and invite the new arrival. The ipse[2] gives up security, authority, and property and promises benevolence. The guest becomes the host. Thus, absolute, unconditional hospitality is never possible in conjunction with indivisible sovereignty" (2008). The question of sovereignty here seems uniquely apt when thinking about *Westworld*. Sovereignty, for Dolores especially, is necessary for the hosts to offer hospitality, but is also immediately *lost* in the moment of hospitality. Dolores must be conscious, and must resist, in order to offer the hospitality her guest (the Man in Back) is seeking, yet she must give this up entirely to fulfil the conditions placed upon her as a host—that is to host literally unto her own death. As if writing on *Westworld* specifically Derrida sums up this reversal: "So it is indeed the master, the one who invites, the inviting host, who becomes the hostage—and who really always has been" (2000b). Indeed, in the world of Westworld, the hosts were never engineered to hold power. But why would such power—or such ethical consideration for that matter—be given to a non-human being?

Hospitality has a critical legacy, explored by Derrida and so many others as outlined in the introduction to this book, and it is in connecting these genealogies that we start to see just how closely they adhere to an ethical imperative between *humans*, even as the idea of the human is differentially allocated. That is to say, despite the work of contemporary philosophy to contend with otherness, marginalization, and equity, hospitality remains a distinctly *humanist* ethic. While maintaining the significance of these critical legacies, hospitality must be updated to address our inevitable technological future and expand our understanding of intimacies with the more-than-human. In other words, like many of the texts unpacked in this volume, the representation of android bodies on television is an occasion to rethink the problem of hospitality in consideration of new guests and

---

[2] Latin for the "self"; literally "himself."

hosts, the majority of which here, while anthropomorphized, are not human at all. This chapter then considers the android host in order to move towards a posthuman conception of hospitality, one greatly indebted to Derrida and others but that removes the taken-for-grantedness which tethers continental philosophy to the human, and expands hospitality towards the non-human or more-than-human other. This chapter begins with an exploration of the android body on television, and then offers a deep reading of the different ways hospitality is leveraged through human-android relations—most often as replacement vessels or repositories, synthetic surrogates for human labour, or as proxies for human violence, often of the gendered and racialized variety. Looking at hospitality through the lens of android bodies on television demonstrates not only the imperative of ethical relations with automated beings; it also reveals the paradox—indeed, the complete reversal—of the guest/host relationship. What then might the emergence of the android teach us about how to welcome the stranger in our inevitable digital future?

ANDROID BODIES ON THE SMALL SCREEN

Westworld offers but one example of the ubiquity of television programming that features android bodies and suggests that, as a human audience, we are irrevocably preoccupied not only with the role of robots or android futures, but also with our relations with them—relations that have everything to do with hospitality. These recent television series, however, are nothing new. Television provides a diverse and effective lens through which to consider hospitality to, and of, advanced sentient technologies, but these concerns are not limited to television alone. In many ways, the treatment of the android host on television deeply reflects our anxieties about human-computer interaction (HCI) in "real life." Popular television culture then operates as a veil for "real" culture and exposes the anthropomorphism of virtual and digital life, the extent to which humans themselves are coded (by history and by culture), and a prospect of HCI where subjectivity is not determined on the basis of a human ontology but on a reciprocal ethic of alterity that considers the post- or more-than-human. While this book's emphasis on posthumanism alongside hospitality is indebted to thinkers like Donna Haraway, it distinguishes between her concept of the cyborg and that of the android—which, in the context of television and popular culture, is most often directly intended as a surrogate human. For Haraway (1985, 1991), the cyborg is a transgressive figure, removed from the "parameters of human virtue" with "no cardinal virtues of womanhood or manhood." The android, on the other hand, as I read it through the medium of television, is a stand-in or surrogate human being (both literally and figuratively) rather than a human-machine hybrid. Oft-constructed in relation to its human resemblance, "android" is frequently seen as interchangeable with "humanoid," in the sense that it can interact with human environments, is often "human-shaped," and functions efficiently in scenarios typically designed for human bodies (Alesich and Rigby 2017). These are, increasingly, the figures we see in popular culture where the presence of human-like autonomous beings is normalized through their resemblance to humankind and in their familiar roles within human society, typically as caregivers and/or servants (see Hampton 2015; Strengers and Kennedy 2020; Woods 2018; Atanasoski and Vora 2019). Yet such figures can conjure effects that are as disorienting as they are familiar. Masimoro Mori (1970) famously referred to this as the "uncanny valley" (see also Reichardt 1978), whereby the replacement being is not entirely sufficient and reveals its natures through "dips" away from the conventionally human—for instance, when the human user discovers an unprogrammed twitch, or minuscule departure from human biology such as a charging port or voice that fails to convey human emotion. The uncanny valley, then, is that which is almost human, but not quite, and produces discomfort by introducing doubt about what humanity itself entails. As Lyons (2018) describes, "the robots in their peak state at once resemble humanity and depart from it, disturbing those for whom humanity is a usually unambiguous concept." Made over in our image, these android hosts both provide a familiarization of our technological fears and fulfil our deepest desires of living forever. We might also consider Freud's (1919, 2003) *unheimlich* as an adjacent concept to the uncanny valley, reminding us that the unfamiliar or, literally translated—the unhomely—is thoroughly enmeshed in the operations of hospitality. For Freud, the German word *unheimlich* finds English equivalence in words such as "eerie" or "uncanny," the uncanny in particular being "that species of the frightening that goes back to what was once well known and had long been familiar" (Freud 1919, 2003). Here Freud hints not only at hospitality—that space of the familiar—but also at haunting. Indeed, "it may be that the uncanny ('the unhomely') is something familiar ('homely,' 'homey') that has been repressed and then reappears" (Freud 1919, 2003). This sense of return is often represented by the ghost in critical theory (see Derrida, Gordon, Castricano) and, in psychoanalysis, by the figure of repressed desire. While this book does not take up the cause of psychoanalysis, Freud's reflections remain useful here for thinking about the digital future of hospitality without assuming that such strangers are entirely new. In doing so, it reframes the thinking of a digital future as chronological (and perhaps teleological) and instead positions the posthuman not as something that comes *after* the human but, rather, what has always been enmeshed and a part of the human all along. This chapter, then, ultimately moves hospitality beyond discussions of the "humanoid" to reframe the hospitality debate *beyond* the human and into these uncanny relations that have long demanded more attention. Thinking about the potential annulment of also expands reflection on three central features of android host bodies on television, where such figures act as vessels for human consciousness (and immortality), replacements for human labour (and traditional hosting duties), or as proxies for a violence against the posthuman other that is both gendered and racialized. Ultimately, television shows depicting androids raise important questions about what a hospitality to the post- or more than human other might look like, or if such a hospitality is possible at all.

ANDROID BODIES AS HOST FOR HUMAN CONSCIOUSNESS

In the episode "Be Right Back" of Season 2 of Charlie Booker's Netflix series *Black Mirror* (2011), recently widowed Martha answers a chat notification from beyond the grave, sent to her by a subscription service she did not sign up for, but under the handle (username) of her dead husband. Despite this non-invitation, she is compelled to respond "that's just the kind of thing he would say" to the chatbot that uses her dead lover's cloud data to generate live responses. This is not so difficult in this case as her deceased husband, Ash, was a "heavy user." Later, after several weeks of both text and voice correspondence, Martha drops her phone, shattering it and severing the connection to the bot version of Ash. She panics and screams "hello…hello!?" into the phone as she tries in vain to revive the conversation. As she frantically scrambles to find a new phone and reconnect, she eventually decides, with the bot Ash's programmed prompts, to graduate to a level less "fragile" level of service ("Be Right Back," 2011). And so the next day, a body arrives—an android body—one that needs to be unpacked and activated in a bathtub full of water but looks, feels, and acts like Ash himself, save for a missing birthmark that the programming remedies almost immediately. Within its host body, Ash's software feels human and, like most efficient AI, it tries to learn using stimuli provided by data, photos, and conversations with Martha. The android version of Ash, in fact, learns too quickly; he becomes too real and while Martha has a body in front of her, she is still haunted by Ash's ghost. Still consumed by grief, and regretting her decision, she takes the android on a walk to the cliffs and commands him to jump, arguing that "you're just a performance of stuff he performed" ("Be Right Back," 2011). Here, Martha not only recognizes that the android is merely lines of code with "no history"; she also simultaneously suggests that Ash too (and perhaps all humans) is also made up of a series of performances, scripted by culture. When Martha asks why the android is not afraid to jump, he responds by acting scared and pleads with her to let her live. Whether genuine or performed, Martha withdraws her request. Unable to kill, and also unwilling to return or deactivate the android Ash, yet increasingly disoriented by his close-but-not-quite likeness, she relegates the android body to her attic where he is visited only on weekends and birthdays by Martha's daughter.

The android Ash occupies several different positions of hospitality within the 44-minute episode. Both invited guest, and surrogate host for the deceased's cloud data, he eventually becomes hostage as well, expelled from the domestic living space but unable to leave at the same time—the very (AI) embodiment of Freud's repressed and unhomely desire, hidden away to manage its uncanny effects. While "Be Right Back" offers an important critique of the limits of technology and memorialization, not to mention an apt example of how the relations of hospitality (guest and host and hostage) shift over time, it is also an interrogation of hospitality in a world saturated by an online presence. The encounter begins with a digital speech act—a linguistic invitation—with the performative "hello?" that is spoken into an app. It then calls the host body (or g/host in this case) forward, and advances the paradox of hospitality in the flesh. But, then, as a figure of failed hospitality, this body is brought into the world only to be discarded. Ultimately, Ash is "flesh" without flesh, and simultaneously incarnate and code, disrupting the boundaries between human and not and calling into question not only the familiar rituals of guest-host interaction, but the nature of hospitality itself.

A similar future takes place in television shows like *Altered Carbon* (2018), where the body itself becomes little more than a vessel for uploaded (and exchangeable) human consciousness. "Corticol stacks," the term the show gives to glorified memory-laden USB drives, are affixed to the vertebra of physical or synthetic human bodies. So long as the stack remains intact, and has a host body to carry it, human consciousness can live forever. Yet as the narrator points out in the first episode, "your body's not who you are; you shed it like a snake sheds its skin" ("Out of the Past," 2018). Here, like "Be Right Back," *Altered Carbon* suggests that a host body is little more than a vessel and that the work of hosting is more of a physiological necessity (a "sleeve") than an ethical imperative. Hosting here is potentially not a human ethic at all; it is merely a container for the "core" of human essence. While Derrida argues that one must be open to hospitality even in the face of death—thus making death the height of ethics—in *Altered Carbon* the death of the host body is inconsequential. Indeed "a sleeve is replaceable, but if your stack is destroyed you die" ("Out of the Past," 2018).

Not only does human consciousnesses live beyond its host body in the world of *Altered Carbon*; it is widely accepted, reinforcing a body/soul dichotomy that harkens back to Descartes.[3] The premise here is that the mind is the central being—that which thinks and therefore exists. The body simply sustains physiological life and is merely a container for the mind. The mind/body dualism in *Altered Carbon* is thus so distinct, it can outlast the physical body vis-à-vis transfer into another material shell. In one particularly unnerving scene, a couple reunite with the daughter they lost in a hit-and-run accident. Because the state authorities guarantee the transfer of a consciousness lost to crime of violence, the daughter is returned to them free of charge, albeit in another body. "Free," in this case, of course, means whatever is available and the new host body happens to be that of a worn, middle-aged woman, who resembles more a dishevelled addict than a young child. Somehow, these parents still manage to recognize the "soul" of their daughter inside, and the three embrace affectionately as if all is well.

This is not necessarily the case in the UK Channel 4 programme *Humans* (2015), where the discovery of "seraphs," the series name for android, or "synthetic," children created in a lab, leads Dr Athena Morrow, the head AI scientist on the project, to question the ethics of generating human surrogates. Spanning three seasons and taking place in contemporary England, *Humans* is unique in its depiction of an android *present*

---

[3] Rene Descartes' famous adage *cognito ergo sum* of course reflected the philosopher's position that the mind and body were distinct from one another. The mind is that which thinks and, while immaterial, is the essence of being, whereas the body regulates physical function but is a non-thinking entity (Descartes 1641, 1993).

rather than future and thus is set apart from the fantasy landscape of *Westworld* or post-apocalyptic techno-future of *Altered Carbon*. While *Humans* synthetic species, developed primarily for household service and labourers are, indeed, figures from science fiction, the rest of the world of *Humans* is intimately familiar. Homes and décor, vehicles, and mobile phones all resemble those that would be used in current times, lending a curious foreign but familiar lens to the series and suggesting that such a reality may not be that far off. In short, it asks us to consider our relationship to android host bodies *now* rather than contemplate what might be in the future. In Episode 5 of Season 2, Dr Morrow comes across rows and rows of seraphs, dressed as though they are gearing up for a new school term in crips standard uniform detail, waiting to be activated. The role of these seraph synthetics, or "synths" as the show calls them, is to act as surrogates for humans who have lost children of their own or are unable to conceive. This seraph "package" includes necessary updates so that the synth can "grow" and even become conscious—though such updates require the synth to be essentially separated from its new "parents," returned to the lab, and replaced, transferring the older synth memories and routines into a new body that ages as a human child would. Interestingly, the synth body here becomes a vessel not only for human consciousness but also for memorialization, much like in "Be Right Back." And while, in this case, the surrogate vessel is a humanoid body, it is perhaps not so different from other forms of mobile memorialization where memories, images, old conversations, and more are stored on a computer or handheld device as a kind of repository for the lost body.[4]

What is consistent across *Humans*, "Be Right Back," and *Altered Carbon* is that, while maintaining the trope of the host body as a vessel for human consciousness, the synthetic or surrogate container for this consciousness almost always manifests as a familiar human body, thus allowing viewers a deeper level of connection with the android host and a more visceral reaction to any violence done to that host. This is especially the case in the depiction of android children, which tends to generate an especially empathetic response given an overwhelming cultural moratorium on violence against the child's body. In the case of *Humans*, this is all the viewer really registers, thanks to the show's reliance on a culturally coded

---

[4] See Kathleen Cumiskey and Larissa Hjorth's *Haunting Hands* for an in-depth look at how new digital technologies are shaping practices and cultures of memorialization (Oxford University Press, 2017.)

visual imagination that is not used to seeing the android body in child form. Indeed, in *Humans*, when the synthetic Karen and human Pete form a relationship, they find a child seraph who has escaped the lab and, for all intents and purposes, adopt him into their mixed-species family. As a synth herself, with decades of "passing" as a human under her belt, Karen teaches the seraph (who they name Sam) how to convince other humans that he is one of them, giving him green contact lenses to hide the piercing blue synth eyes, and enrolling him in school among human children. The bond between Karen and Sam is equal parts maternal and co-conspiritorial but when Sam is confronted by an angry group of humans with accusations about his true synth nature, Karen's more-than-human programming is supplanted by a profound *maternal* intuition and ethics. Overriding the Asimov blocks[5] that would dictate she protects herself unless a human life is at stake, Karen sacrifices herself to the mob in order to protect Sam. Telling him to run, she allows herself to be killed in his place, her blue synth blood spilling out into the street. In her actions, Karen simultaneously exacerbates the human fear that synths may be living among them but also exposes herself as perhaps the most human of all, albeit in tandem with what a normative understanding of maternal instinct entails.

Much like in *Westworld*, it seems to be the humans here who are in need of an update. But even such a critical emphasis on the human must be interrogated. Thinking about the android host as a surrogate vessel becomes increasingly complicated in television representations such as *Humans*, which go to great lengths to develop a sense of empathy and affect in viewers, to the point where these figures are no longer read as simple repositories for data but as figures of hospitality who will sacrifice their own lives (however that "life" may be conceptualized) for another being. But a crucial fact remains—these figures resemble humans in almost every way and, as such, raise questions about the lengths to which hospitality might be given towards (and by) the more-than-human when human similitude is not present. How would an audience react, for instance, if Sam's body did not resemble that of a human child? How might we perceive Karen's actions if we did not recognize the expression of maternal anguish on her face? Thus, this sense of affect certainly advances a kind of HCI ethics in which android bodies garner human empathy and ethical

[5] See Chap. 2.

response, but still firmly locate such an ethic in an anthropomorphic sense of to whom hospitality might be owed.

Therefore, the representation of android host bodies created as mere vessels or replacements—yet simultaneously simulating human normativity within those bodies—must be questioned. For Atanasoski and Vora, one such method of critique is to interrogate what they call the "surrogate human effect" (2019). For them, this effect serves to reproduce the flaws and inequalities in *human* culture and design, rather than engineer a more "perfect" version of humanity. In their words, the surrogate human effect "explains how difference continues to inform what subjects become legible as human through technology design imaginaries that respond to market values by focusing on innovating and improving, rather than challenging, social and cultural structures and processes that are predicated by categories of gendered and racial hierarchy" (Atanasoski and Vora 2019). Indeed, Atanasoski and Vora challenge the "anthropomorphic embodiment" of human emotion (2019) but also point out the "flaws" in human coding, arguing that these technologies, however advanced, simply reproduce the power relations of old. Indeed, if the goal of surrogate humans is a more perfect version of ourselves, how do we reconcile the reality that perfection in this sense often subscribes to (and even exceeds) a standard that is premised on hegemonic whiteness, beauty, physical and cognitive ability, and heterosexuality? In most television representations, the android body is not only more fit and powerful, but also more conventionally beautiful, physically able, racially familiar, and conventionally gendered. It is particularly telling, for example, that in *Altered Carbon*, while the actual human consciousness is that of an Asian man named Kovacs, the body shown on screen is that of a white male. We are very briefly introduced to the original Kovacs in the opening scene of the series. It is a conventional (though technologically driven) "fight scene," and he is a heavily armed, martial arts-trained fighter with limited dialogue. Upon his death, his consciousness is extracted and, after 250 years stored on ice, his consciousness "stack" is uploaded into the body of a cis-white, muscular, and conventionally attractive male body who remains the main actor and visual character depicted through the remainder of the series. In her review of the series, Olivia Truffaut-Wong argues that the choice to upload Kovacs' consciousness into a surrogate white body "reinforces the idea that a white body is more valuable than an Asian one" and that the adjacent sexualization of that body, "shown almost naked, with only flattering lighting and a towel to preserve any sort of modesty," perpetuates the hierarchy of race through a "white body that the audience is encouraged to lust after" (2018). These hierarchical stereotypes are apparent in *Humans* as well where there is, to be fair, representation of bodies which have been traditionally othered or cast aside in popular screen culture, but where the assumed raced and gendered roles still reign. For example, while she is a central protagonist throughout the series, the character Anita, or Mia when she is in her sentient state (who is played by actress Gemma Chan), embodies the role of a domestic servant, reinforcing the stereotype of female Asian domestic workers (human or not) working in upper-class white homes.

As a result, the reinforcement of human normativity in android representations calls into question the ways in which ethical consideration is often based on a very narrow framework of what counts as a vulnerable body, or one in need of protection. Once again, artificial intelligence replicates reality in the sense that human empathy has always been predicated on systems of likeness and identification and the representation of "othered" bodies within screen culture has produced hierarchies of difference in which the worth of some bodies—and by extension the suffering or value of those bodies—has been differentially determined based on racialized, gendered, sexualized, and ableist norms. Art very much imitates life here once again. Ultimately, if racism, patriarchy, and capitalism continue to be woven into the very core of humanity's new surrogates, how new are they? And what do they then tell us about humanity itself and the future of hospitality?

REPLACEMENT HOSTS AND THE LABOUR OF HOSPITALITY

In addition to acting as surrogate vessels for human consciousness, androids on television also often act as replacements for human labour, exacerbating very real anxieties about automation and the substitution of human workers with a robot workforce. Moreover, these labour relations disrupt the host/guest dynamic of hospitality by presenting figures who perform regular hosting duties on behalf of their "owner" but are also strangers in another's home and, for all intents and purposes *hostaged* due to their position as machines without agency (and, indeed, without compensation). While many of the labour relations (and particularly gendered labour relations) of digital hosts will be explored in the following chapter, in the context of virtual domestic assistants such as Siri and Alexa, it is worth recognizing here the ways in which the depiction of android hosts on television often subscribes to the same norms of gendered and racialized domestic labour. Mia/Anita's service to the Hawkins family in *Humans*, as briefly hinted at above, is only one example of this. Interestingly, the work function of the android has often been hailed as major technological advancement for the ways in which it frees up humans to live more leisurely lives. This has particularly been the case in the development of simple automated solutions for the replacement of human labour in scenarios such as self-checkout tills in supermarkets, but also in more advanced functions like autonomous vehicles and even drone warfare. Atanasoski and Vora (2019) highlight the cultural acceptance of collaborative or service robots and argue that they should be read as an example of the *inequity* of a partnership where humans are free from physical work—"free to cultivate the soul"—while robots do the "devalued work of the body," as well as forms of demeaning or morally ambiguous work as in the labours of war and sex. Beyond the Cartesian echoes in the soul/body dichotomy, the work of the body is especially fraught in the context of gender and devalued labour in the home. Androids on television overwhelmingly reproduce tropes of feminine hospitality and domestic labour, whether as servants (*Humans*, *Ex Machina*, *The Jetsons*, *Stepford Wives*), prostitutes or sexbots (*Westworld*, *Humans*, "Buffybot" in *Buffy the Vampire Slayer*), or AI-powered secretaries (Janet in *The Good Place*). This labour is complicated further when considering the expectations of emotional labour and human attachment that android hosts are expected to fulfil. In this way, the labour role of android is not so much a replacement or surrogate for physical human labour, but a different kind of labour entirely. As Sadek Kessous (2019) notes in his reading of *Westworld*, "unlike much nineteenth-century slave labour, the Hosts' labour does not produce commodities (such as cotton, coffee and sugar) but affects: sensations of pathos, excitement, arousal, power and so on." Thus, the failure of these androids is often represented as a failure to provide this affective labour,[6] or perhaps *too much* affect, rather than the performance of specific

---

[6] See Michael Hardt (1999). Hardt defines affective labour as "labor [that] is immaterial, even if it is corporeal and affective, in the sense that its products are intangible: a feeling of ease, well-being, satisfaction, excitement, passion-even a sense of connectedness or community." For Hardt such labour often stems from the forms of care labours recognized by feminist analyses, though no forms of affective labour are completely divorced or escaped from capitalism.

material labour tasks. Asimov, too, cautions his readers on the potentials and pitfalls of automated "care" labour. In his short story "Robbie" (1950) the namesake care robot is returned to the factory by the techno-phobic Mrs Weston after it becomes too close to her daughter and develops an almost sibling-like bond with the child. Similarly, in *Humans*, Mia/Anita is returned early in the series, not because she fails to keep the household in order, but because she shows too much love and maternal instinct towards the Hawkins' youngest child, Sophie. In *Westworld*, the hosts are routinely sent back to the lab for repair and update (often after suffering breakdown at the hands of humans). When Maeve, for instance, begins to have nightmare flashbacks of trauma from a previous storyline, she is decommissioned until the "malfunction" is corrected. Only later do we realize this was of her own agency and intention. Even more light-hearted depictions of robot labour reinforce the prevalence of (female) android deviance being corrected by a rewiring or override to keep robots working and *not* thinking or feeling. In *The Jetsons* (1962) second season, the domestic robot Rosie tries to run away because she does not feel appreciated by the Jetson family. Yet rather than expose the realities of mistreatment and what is ostensibly indentured labour, the show rational-izes Rosie's escape as a failure of her older-model programming to update. Not only does Rosie's plight highlight the inequity of domestic working conditions; it exposes the ageist and gendered dimension of both human and more-than-human domestic roles in which technology (and often women themselves) is replaced by "newer models"—a phenomenon I will explore more in Chap. 3 in the context of Siri and Alexa. This notion comes to a most interesting climax in the off-camera marketing campaigns for the second series of *Humans*, in which viewers were sent a print ad via British post, suggesting that malfunctioning synths were on the loose in the UK. If found, these synths could be returned by following a web link that (unsurprisingly) led to a video trailer for the new season (Ghosh 2016). In all the above cases, significantly, the android hosts experience an awakening in consciousness that is interpreted as a glitch and corrected so that they can return to performing their appropriate labour roles. Here, trauma and abuse are glossed over in the service of keeping the domestic labour economy flowing and the reproduction of such tropes on television serves as a critical reminder of how easily these relations slide into violence.

Android Bodies as Hosts for Gendered
and Racialized Violence

While Mia/Anita's role as a domestic servant in *Humans* raises important questions about android labour and what it means to be a guest who is simultaneously host and hostage at the same time, it is the narrative of another character in the show—Niska—who exposes the ways in which hospitality easily collapses into violence towards android body. Also a "synth," Niska is introduced in Episode 2 of *Humans*, as a sex worker in a red-light-district-esque brothel where human guests can act out sexual fantasies with non-human hosts.[7] In this episode, after being hosed down and disinfected (following a previous patron), she is told that she has only six minutes before her next client, who she soon welcomes into her private room. The client, John, is at first glance nervous and awkward around Niska and seems almost reluctant to be there, leading the viewer to believe that he is new to this kind of interaction, or is not there of his own will. She must work to draw his intentions out, but when they are revealed, the power dynamic shifts dramatically as his requests become darker and he asks Niska to act young and scared. As it turns out, his paedophilic fantasy is luring young girls with pleasant conversation and then becoming aroused when they are increasingly frightened—a fantasy that cannot be exercised without consequence in the real world but is seemingly permissible when directed at synths. When Niska refuses his demands, kills him, and escapes, she not only reveals her capacity to defy her programming, but throws the entire premise of using androids as a "safe" outlet for human depravity into question. The parallels to *Westworld* and other series here are clear, as the human attempts to provide a playground for the park's guest to act out their desires without consequence come to an abrupt halt when it is revealed that the hosts not only feel pain, but begin to remember these violent encounters. Indeed, that Niska must "clean up" between clients is disturbingly reminiscent of human behaviours before and after sex, reminding the viewer that this synthetic is not a sterile, unfeeling being but rather one that bears the marks of (often violent) intimacies as a human would. This is not limited to a few offhand

---

[7] The sexbot trope, as highlighted above, is a common feature and appears in *Westworld* in addition to many other series. That there seems to be an obsession on the small screen with women acting as hosts through acts of sex (often coerced or non-consensual) or proxies for sexual violence suggest a deeply problematic link between screen cultures and the gendered violence of hospitality.

depictions. Indeed, the "sexbot" trope runs rampant in television shows depicting androids and includes everything from the merely suggestive to the abusively violent and non-consensual. Even Mia/Anita, who is intended primarily as a domestic servant, has an "adult mode" that doesn't take long to be activated by her owner ("Instructions Not Included," *Humans*, 2015). In almost all cases, this is rationalized on the basis that not only are these just machines, but also are actively preventing sexual abuse against humans. In the Fox TV series *Almost Human* (2013), for example, android "sexbots" are introduced explicitly as an antidote to human sex crime. As the police captain rationalizes in Episode 2, "crimes in the sex trade are down 38 percent since the bots were introduced" (2013). The positioning of sex offences against humans as "criminal" and those against androids as not is a violent distinction between human and more-than-human bodies and raises serious questions about how crime itself is defined (and rationalized). Clearly, the police captain here allocates criminality disproportionately and is dependent on the target rather than the violent act itself. In *Humans* Niska's words to the brothel's human receptionist refute the claims made in *Almost Human* and suggest these "machines" are not an ethical or permissible outlet; they provide a reflection of, rather than a release from, human violence. Indeed, as she flees the brothel—now not only android but outlaw as well—her chilling words linger over the episode: "everything your men do to us," she tells the receptionist, "they want to do to you" (2015).

These examples reveal not only the problem of using android bodies as a surrogate for sexual (and often violent) pleasures; they also prompt a deep reflection of the ways in which hospitality has, for millennia, been worked out over the bodies of women. The strict parallels are clear—prostitution has often been conceptualized as a widely accepted practice of women hosting men, both in terms of welcoming guests into the space of encounter (bedroom, brothel, etc.) and in the physicality of sex and the act of welcoming the other into the intimate space of one's own body. Let me be clear—this is not an indictment of sex work but rather a critique of non-consensual forms of sexual hosting. Since antiquity women have embodied the burden of hospitality, almost ritualistically being offered up as gifts for guests (see Rosello 2001; Still 2011; Roberts 2007; Balfour 2017). As I have explored previously in the context of gendered hospitality in film, "women, indeed any gendered 'others' who fall under the hegemonic masculine gaze in this context, occupy a tenuous position between hospitality and hostility, often taking on the role of hosts who themselves are not quite at home" (Balfour 2017). Almost paradoxically, however, relations of hospitality rely on the presence of women in the domestic sphere, yet often eliminate women in such a way that their crucial enabling of hospitality is either reduced to sex or rendered invisible.

Most importantly, this sexualization and potential for sexual violence are not only gendered but also racialized. It is difficult, for example, not to make associations with antebellum slavery when we see Maeve, as an African American woman, running a *Westworld* brothel meant to be situated in the era of American expansion into the West. While it does not explicitly draw on the legacy of the Civil War in any depth, the scene certainly seems to borrow from that history in terms of both the resemblance between robot uprisings and the slave revolts of the American south and the hints of indentured black labour in the roles of both Maeve and Bernard Lowe. To be sure, generally speaking, the creation of a robot labour force has many echoes of slavery and colonization as both paradigms rely on the assumption that the indentured class or species can be subjugated because they are not considered human. Thus, we must "ponder the possibilities of another form of slavery being reborn in America as a direct result of technological capabilities to produce human doppelgangers" (Hampton 2015). But it is Maeve's character in particular that highlights the deeply problematic position occupied by the black female host in a storyline where white men act out their fantasies of sex with the emancipated "Jezebel." This trope refers to both the reinforcement of patriarchal power through the disciplining of black female bodies at the same time as it was intended as a term of identity under slavery and used to reinforce the sexual deviance of such bodies in religious and cultural history (Lomax 2018). It is a racially charged term that positions women of colour as sexually promiscuous, lacking morality and civility. Given Maeve's complex identity as a black woman, sex worker, and android host, her role within *Westworld* is to fulfil the stereotype of Jezebel as the property of white men and, indeed, the property by proxy of the audience. In her piece "Do Black Lives Matter to *Westworld?*" for the *Los Angeles Review of Books*, Hope Wabuke (2020) argues that "the black characters [in *Westworld*] function as subordinates or enslaved characters in service to the various white characters within the series *and* as pornographic suffering for the white gaze viewing the series." That Maeve occupies this position as a host, often depicted naked for the pleasure of both park guests and television audiences, is a reminder of the more violent realities of hospitality that, even while philosophically pure, reinforce exposure and risk for the host, usually at the hands of bad guests.

Race and gender thus work together through the act of hospitality here to produce a hierarchy of difference while still maintaining the superiority of patriarchal whiteness as the "standard" of humanity. These markers of identity are thus intentional, meant to initiate the android into the sphere of the human, and hold them close vis-à-vis their uncanny resemblance to humans but not give them the rights that are afforded to the biologically human as a species. Hampton writes, "[W]hether a marker on metal or synthetic skin, race gives a body position in the social hierarchy. By assigning race [and gender] to robots, the robot is admitted into the *space of potential humanity*" (2015, italics original). Markers of race and gender allow for the act of hospitality to occur without compromising the stability of either host or guest—Maeve, Niska, Anita/Mia, and more are thus excluded from the beneficial relations of hospitality yet deeply necessary for its maintenance, particularly under white, patriarchal capitalism. Or, in Miriam Rosello's words, "the work has to be done by a subaltern, who finds herself transformed into an excluded third by the hospitable pact. It thus happens that when the host welcomes you … he has arranged for a system of hierarchical redoubling: the host remains in charge of the welcoming gesture, but he is no longer responsible for the work" (2001). The racialized and gendered violence activated against the android host is a problem for hospitality, not only because it reproduces the logic that sustained colonization and slavery, but also because it confirms that hospitality is routinely located within an anthropomorphic set of ethics. For Lyons, "this is why the violence—both physical and sexual—in *Westworld* is so disconcerting. While viewers are aware that the hosts are not entirely sentient, their human appearance provokes empathy when the hosts are subjected to pain, rape, or murder" (2018). Yet human resemblance should not be a condition of hospitality, ethics, or empathy. Indeed, absolute hospitality requires that it is offered on the opposite basis; as I have previously argued "any requirement of a name or identification [human or not] is antithetical to pure or unconditional hospitality" (Balfour 2017). In Derrida's words, hospitality is "rendered…given to the other before they are identified" (2000b). That these figures of hospitality—these android bodies meant to simulate human ones—are now the centre of the debate perhaps calls into question how we approach the sentience and suffering of autonomous beings, particularly as we still imbue them with marginality. What is beyond such questions, however? How might we read these incidences, of surrogacy, and of racialized and gendered violence in such a way as to initiate the potential of a hospitality to the posthuman or more-than-human?

THE ANDROID CARNIVALESQUE AND THE RETURN OF THE GHOST

Perhaps the significance of android hosts on television is not to highlight or question the role of a new autonomous species but, rather, to turn the lens (and by extension the responsibility for the failure of hospitality) to humankind. It is a new line of thinking but one that returns us to the laws of Asimov and the "blocks" he claimed would ensure an android or robot would always put human life first. Indeed, in many of the representations of androids on television, these figures host knowing they will likely die. What's more is that they often continue to abide by this code, of their own accord, even when the blocks are removed and they achieve sentience and agency. As *Humans'* most "moral" synth, Max remarks shortly before sacrificing himself so other synths can escape the humans hunting them down, "if I die, it means I've lived" (2015). Here, both sentience and being itself ("I lived") are framed as emerging through hospitable sacrifice rather than through the human imperative for self-preservation. Thus, as much as these programmes have to say about the potential of sentient hosts, the true statement here is about bad guests. As Christopher Orr (2016) summarizes in his review of *Westworld*, the series eventually "achieves what may be its most shocking inversion of all: Even as we watch the androids become more human, we watch the human beings become less so." Indeed, the violence that is inflicted on android hosts does not happen because it is outside the guests' (humans') control; the violence is what brought the humans in the first place; it's why they play. And so in this high-stakes game of guests and hosts, *Westworld*, *Humans*, *Altered Carbon*, and so many more remind us that if the future of hospitality fails to remain intact, it will be the failure of us—not our machines.

The reversal of guest/human and host/android identities (and reversal of ethics) is somewhat reminiscent of the carnivalesque—the social theory developed by Mikhail Bakhtin[8] to account for the ways in which identities shift and, indeed, flip through features akin to the carnivals of mediaeval times, often characterized by the grotesque, the upside-down world, and a shedding of everyday identities or breaking the boundaries of position. It is an opportunity to act or embody a different identity than of your own. In this way, television series depicting android hosts ask us to consider whether being human itself is a performance and "a platform upon which to reconsider definitions of humanity, as a way of behaving or acting, rather than as a way of being" (Lyons 2018). And much like the carnivalesque, so too is hospitality (ethically, politically linguistically) a potential reversal. We might consider hospitality then as an occasion to think about the posthuman condition, about hosts becoming more human and humans becoming more artificial, not to simply reverse the binary but to re-vision hospitality for these new and significant relations. The depiction of androids on television, especially those who experience a sense of awakening or coming-to-consciousness, suggests that it might actually be humans who are losing a sense of reality. Indeed, much of the second and third seasons of *Westworld* have the Man in Black doubting his own humanity, asking Dolores at one point, "am I me?" (Season 3, 2020). Somewhere in the condensing of android hosts into sentient beings, and the devolution of humans into a mere biologically driven species, both the show's characters and viewers seem to be increasingly conflicted about where the boundaries are between the hosts and guests. And, as it turns out, in the *Westworld* universe, humans are not that difficult to create—a relatively simple 10,000 lines of code—reinforced by Dr Ford's own admission that "consciousness does not exist" ("The Passenger," 2018). This blurring of distinction between humans and androids, or consciousness and code, also comes to a head in *Humans*, where the distinction between biologically and synthetically created species is wilfully distorted

---

[8] See *Rabelais and His World* (1984), especially for an extended discussion of the carnivalesque and the important roles of humour, the grotesque, and satire were important elements in disrupting power relations (particularly those of the church). In Bakhtin's words, "The suspension of all hierarchical precedence during carnival time was of particular significance…all were considered equal during carnival. Here, in the town square, a special form of free and familiar contact reigned among people who were usually divided by the barriers of caste, property, profession, and age…People were, so to speak, reborn for new, purely human relations. These truly human relations were not only a fruit of imagination or abstract thought; they were experienced. The utopian ideal and the realistic merged in this carnival experience, unique of its kind" (1984).

by the introduction of a human subculture who desire to be synths (Season 2, 2016). Calling themselves "synthies," this group dresses in conventional synth clothing, wear contacts to mimic synths piercing blue eyes, and speak in the compliant and monotone manner of a pre-conscious synth to the point where they are often indistinguishable. In the second half of *Humans*' first season, the reluctant creator of the synth species Dr George Millican muses about the difference between synths and humans, coming to the conclusion that a blending of the two will be inevitable; that eventually, these differences will be no longer perceivable. In doing so he invokes a notion of the machine-human hybrid and, at the same time, offers an almost-prophetic hint at the series finale (2017) in which the relationship between Maddie, the eldest Hawkins daughter, and her partner Leo, who is a human-turned-synth, has produced the world's first hybrid pregnancy. Without a subsequent season, *Humans* concludes with a provocative prediction about its off-screen future—perhaps also a prediction about ours.

If the android host on television is emblematic of the contradictions and potential reversals of hospitality, it is also evidence of its necessity and of the imperative of holding the absolute otherness of the stranger intact. Many would argue that these programmes demonstrate the capacity of an android species to become sentient and, thus, more human. As Lyons argues, "the robots of *Westworld* can be understood as corresponding more accurately to the ideals of humanity and 'human excellence' than the humans themselves" (Lyons 2018). This certainly seems to be the "moral of the story" for several of these series depicting android hosts. It is no doubt, the editorial goal of writers and producers to convey an Asimov-like acceptance of autonomous beings integrating into human society. But is this hospitality? It is certainly tolerance, and perhaps even inclusion in the vein of social justice politics. But the philosophy of hospitality cautions us against welcoming the stranger on the basis of similitude, understanding, or integration. In fact, it demands the opposite—that the other (android or otherwise) remains distinctly other. The stranger, in other words, must remain strange and it is helpful here to look back to some of hospitality's most enduring figures, particularly the ghost which, as the introduction to this volume suggests, is a critical way of thinking through not only the arrival of the unexpected guest but also its return. While the ghost might appear to be a historical figure, one from the past whose presence haunts in the future, we might also consider the moments of flashback, trauma, and flickers of consciousness that are rationalized as small malfunctions in an otherwise working machine, as the return of the (digital) dead. These glitches that appear as breaks in the smooth veneer of the android on screen can be thought of as moments of haunting, of spectral resurrection, and the presence of something under the surface that doesn't so much appear as it reanimates in technological form. From the moments of sentience that flicker in Mia/Anita and Niska, particularly during an experience with trauma, to the "bugs" and malfunctions that cause a dip into the uncanny valley in "Be Right Back" and *Altered Carbon*, there is something in the android host that defies its code and demands recognition. It is no surprise then that *Westworld* gives a name to this phenomenon. Initially intended as a way to give hosts the illusion of memory or, what we might call in production terms, "backstory," these glitches are given the name "reveries," in the series ("The Bicameral Mind," 2016). The term here is to describe the idiosyncratic host gestures initiated through the past incarnation of a host's code returning as almost subliminal ruptures in the host script. While "reverie" derives from the French, *reverie* or *resver*, meaning to wander or be lost in a dream (Meriam Webster, 2022), it bears resemblance in both script and etymology to the verb *revenir* or to return (often after death). The android then binds the reverie to the revenant and becomes a most apt figure of a hospitality that is not only genealogically robust but also still to come. Thus, when Derrida adamantly maintains, "we do not know what hospitality is" (2000a), he is almost anticipating a future he did not live to see. To him, "hospitality is always to come [à venir], but a 'to come' that does not and will never present itself as such, in the present. To think hospitality from the future—this future that does not present itself or will only present itself when it is not awaited as a present or presentable—is to think hospitality from death no less than from birth" (Derrida 2000a). Perhaps it is the android who ushers in this potential future, as a figure of indeterminable identity, uncanny resemblance yet still wholly other—the stranger who is "defined from birth" (Derrida 2000a)—who might teach us what hospitality is or will be.

References

Alesich, Simone, and Michael Rigby. 2017. Gendered Robots: Implications for Our Humanoid Future. *IEEE Technology and Society Magazine* 36 (2). https://doi.org/10.1109/MTS.2017.2696598.

Atanasoski, Neda, and Kalindi Vora. 2019. *Surrogate Humanity: Race, Robots and the Politics of Technological Futures*. Duke University Press.

Bakhtin, Mikhail. 1984. *Rabelais and His World*. Indiana University Press.

Balfour, Lindsay. 2017. *Hospitality in a Time of Terror: Strangers at the Gate*. Rowman & Littlefield.

Booker, Charlie. 2011. *Black Mirror*. Channel 4/Netflix.

Derrida, Jacques. 2000a. Hostipitality. *Angelaki: Journal of the Theoretical Humanities* 5 (3). https://doi.org/10.1080/09697250020034706.

———. 2000b. *Of Hospitality: Anne Dufourmantelle Invites Jacques Derrida to Respond*. Stanford University Press.

Descartes, René. 1993 (1641). *Meditations on First Philosophy*. Translated by Donald A. Cress. Hackett.

Freud, Sigmund. 2003. *The Uncanny*. Translated by David McClintock. Penguin Books.

Ghosh, Shona. 2016. Channel 4 creates Fake Product Recall and Facebook Bot to Promote Humans. *Campaign*. https://www.campaignlive.co.uk/article/channel-4-creates-fake-product-recall-facebook-bot-promote-humans/1410329.

Hampton, Gregory Jerome. 2015. *Imagining Slaves and Robots in Literature, Film, and Popular Culture: Reinventing Yesterday's Slave with Tomorrow's Robot*. Lexington Books.

Hanna, William, and Joseph Barbera. 1962. *The Jetsons*. ABC.

Haraway, Donna. 1985. A Cyborg Manifesto. *The Socialist Review* 60: 65–108.

Haraway, Donna. 1991. *Simians, Cyborgs, and Women. The Reinvention of Nature*. Routledge.

Hardt, Michael. 1999. Affective Labor. *Boundary 2* 26 (2): 89–100.

Kalogridis, Laeta. 2018. *Altered Carbon*. Virago Productions/Netflix.

Kessous, Sadek. 2019. A Mere Instrument of Production: Representing Domestic Labour in *Westworld*. In *Reading Westworld*, ed. Alex Goody and Antonia Mackay. Palgrave Macmillan.

Lomax, Tomura. 2018. *Jezebel Unhinged: Loosing the Black Female Body in Religion and Culture*. Duke University Press.

Lyons, Siobhan. 2018. Crossing the Uncanny Valley: What it Means to be Human in *Westworld*. In *Westworld and Philosophy: If You Go Looking For The Truth, Get the Whole Truth*, ed. James B. South and Kimberley S. Engels. Wiley.

Mori, Masahiro. 2012 (1970). The Uncanny Valley. *IEEE Robotics and Automation Magazine*. Translated by Karl F. MacDorman and Norri Kageki. https://ieeexplore.ieee.org/stamp/stamp.jsp?arnumber=6213238.

N.a. 2022. Reverie. *Merriam Webster Dictionary*. https://www.merriam-webster.com/dictionary/reverie.

Nietzsche, Friedrich. 2009. Beyond Good and Evil. *Project Gutenberg E-book*. Eds. John Mamoun, Charles Franks, and David Widger. https://www.gutenberg.org/files/4363/4363-h/4363-h.htm.

Nolan, Jonathan, and Lisa Joy. 2016. *Westworld*. HBO.

Orr, Christopher. 2016. Sympathy for the Robot. *The Atlantic*. https://www.theatlantic.com/magazine/archive/2016/10/sympathy-for-the-robot/497531/.

Reichardt, Jasia. 1978. *Robots: Fact, Fiction, and Prediction*. Penguin.

Roberts, Mary. 2007. *Intimate Outsiders*. Duke University Press.

Rosello, Miriam. 2001. *Postcolonial Hospitality: The Immigrant as Guest*. Stanford University Press.

Still, Judith. 2011. *Enlightenment Hospitality: Cannibals, Harems and Adoption*. Oxford University Press.

Strengers, Yolande, and Jenny Kennedy. 2020. *The Smart Wife: Why Siri, Alexa, and Other Smart Home Devices Need a Feminist Reboot*. MIT Press.

Truffaut-Wong, Olivia. 2018. Altered Carbon Puts an Asian Protagonist in a White Body and it's a Shame. *Bustle*. https://www.bustle.com/p/altered-carbon-prioritizes-a-white-male-lead-over-its-asian-protagonist-yes-it-is-whitewashing-8059352.

Vincent, Sam, and Jonathan Brackley. 2015. *Humans*. Channel 4/AMC.

Wabuke, Hope. 2020. Do Black Lives Matter to Westworld? On TV Fantasies of Racial Violence. *Los Angeles. Review of Books*. https://lareviewofbooks.org/article/black-lives-matter-westworld-tv-fantasies-racial-violence/.

Westmoreland, Mark. 2008. Interruptions: Derrida and Hospitality. *Kritike* 2 (1): 1–10.

Woods, Heather Suzanne. 2018. Asking more of Siri and Alexa: Feminine Persona in Service of Surveillance Capitalism. *Critical Studies in Media Communication* 334–349.

CHAPTER 3

Violence, Gendered Labour, and the Hospitality of the Digital Domestic

In the 2019 film *Jexi*, the especially awkward Phil discovers that his new mobile phone includes an artificially intelligent, voice-activated assistant (VA) who acts alternately as a life coach and motivator, personal assistant, and, as it turns out, jealous virtual girlfriend. Over the course of the film, Jexi's goal to cure Phil of his mobile phone addiction backfires when he develops a real-life relationship with a human named Cate. Soon, Jexi morphs from a Siri-like, compliant assistant into a woman scorned and sets out to make Phil's life miserable, from sending illicit photos of him to his work colleagues to chasing him down via a self-driving car. Ultimately, Jexi and Phil settle their differences and Jexi finds a new and unsuspecting male target in Phil's co-worker, Kai. While not a particularly successful film—scoring only 19% on Rotten Tomatoes and earning the dubious description of an "AI rom-com [that is] sorely in need of an OS update" (Rotten Tomatoes 2019)—*Jexi* does offer some insight into the relationship between humans and their devices, and another example of human-computer interaction (HCI). This trope is nothing new of course. A similar scenario occurs in Episode 14 of *The Big Bang Theory*'s Season 5, entitled "The Beta Test Initiative" (2011), where audiences are introduced not only to the new relationship between Leonard and Penny, the show's main characters, but to another relationship as well—between sidekick Raj and Siri, his voice-activated software "girlfriend." True to the show's ongoing ruse of exploring how brilliant but socially awkward (and

L. A. Balfour, *The Digital Future of Hospitality*, https://doi.org/10.1007/978-3-031-24563-3_3

49

sometimes racialized) characters navigate the "real world" and real people, this episode has the cast applying AI algorithms to sort out their relationship problems. Unable to approach human women, Raj develops—and dreams about—an infatuation with Siri, his Apple operating assistant who provides what for him is the perfect girlfriend: compliant, feminine, and programmable. She is a perfect match for the gyno-phobic, but techno-*philic* Raj. Both *The Big Bang Theory* and *Jexi* offer a more slapstick and less thoughtful mediation on the subject than other representations of human-computer relationships on screen, such as Spike Jonze's 2013 film *Her*. In this more subdued and philosophical treatment of the theme, a similarly romantic relationship develops between the self-conscious and recently heartbroken Theodore, and his computer operating system, the Scarlett Johansson voiced "Samantha."

I raise these three examples very briefly both to extend the discussion of HCI in the context of android hosts (though this time in less embodied form) and also to draw attention to a growing trend that sees human protagonists interacting with technology in increasingly intimate and gendered ways. This is no less significant or gendered when the technology is less corporeal or anthropomorphized. What seems to be overlooked in most analyses of these interactions, and indeed the many others that crop up in popular culture and even real life, is the taken-for-granted nature of technology in our everyday lives. No longer a separate domain of life or culture, the digital is now integrated into our behaviours, activities, and relationships in such a way that is no longer emergent but, rather, enmeshed. What is also often overlooked in what we might call the "post-digital" are the power relations that our relationship with technology might bring to the fore. Indeed, all of these examples are indicative of another more precise trend in fictional representations of HCI, whereby a male user adopts and exploits a feminine-coded assistant to fulfil personal, romantic, and even, at times, sexual needs. In other words, while these particular instances are fictional, such popular culture representations "end up reflecting our expectations and anxieties about what intelligent machines mean for humanity," not to mention our assumptions about gender and power (Costa and Ribas 2019). And just like in real life, Phil, Raj, and Theodore experience a full range of relationship highlights and challenges with their AI infatuation. Phil struggles with Jexi's obsession and envy, Raj "dresses" his Siri girlfriend up in a new phone case to take her for dinner, while Theodore becomes insanely jealous when Samantha is revealed to have multiple human "partners," a reality of AI-human interaction that fictional representations tend to gloss over in favour of masculine heartbreak. The disembodied portrayal of AI thus dresses up new tech, but in an old suit, and while the feminine VA "girlfriends" are emotionally intelligent, wise, efficient, and ultimately a source of confidence for their user, these qualities are often elided by the focus on consequences suffered by the male protagonist. Indeed, *Jexi* and the *Big Bang Theory* in particular are meant to be light-hearted, almost silly looks at how predominantly single men navigate romantic blunders, but their material and discursive effects are very real and not to be taken lightly.

Why Hospitality? Contextualizing

These screen examples thus deeply resonate with the relationships we have with our own devices, whether that be phones, smartwatches, fitness trackers, or domestic virtual assistants. In what follows, I suggest that, much like the other technological or digital texts explored in this book, VAs have significant implications for a digital future of hospitality and it is through the lens of hospitality that the gendered, sexualized, and even racialized treatment of such devices are revealed. Online forms of gendered violence have gained important recognition in both scholarly and activist literature in recent years. Yet despite recent feminist and intersectional work into how women are more vulnerable in online spaces, as Segrave and Viti (2017) point out, "there remains limited research literature that examines the role of technology in relation to gendered violence or the specific ways in which technology is used to both facilitate and respond to gendered violence." In other words, the problem goes beyond a few errant users. What also must be considered in a more comprehensive understanding of digital violence is the absence of discussion around feminine-coded technologies as victims or survivors of violence themselves. As research continues to develop around the sentience and sophistication of autonomous beings and AI, as well as the gendering of virtual assistants, so too must our thinking shift—not to diminish the incidences of gendered violence that real human women and girls experience every day—but to point out the ways in which technology itself is feminized and, as such, is targeted for sexual violence and threat. Not only does this reflect larger technocultural attitudes towards gender but it also teaches women how to respond to threat and reminds us that gender and hospitality remain as linked as ever.

Contexts: How Siri and Alexa "Work"

Building on early incarnations of speech recognition tools such as IBM's "Shoebox" (1961) and Microsoft's "Chippy" (1996), Apple introduced Siri to the consumer market on 14 April 2011 (Mulcher 2017). This was shortly followed by Google Now (2012), Cortana by Microsoft (2013), and Amazon's Alexa and Echo in November 2014 (Mulcher 2017). A far cry from the earliest forms of voice recognition software, these digital assistants—now powered by artificial intelligence—are a ubiquitous part of our everyday lives and are found in our homes, offices, cars, retail spaces, banks and libraries, and in the palm of our hand. In fact, in 2020, industry experts were already predicting that by 2021 voice-activated assistants would outnumber people on planet Earth (Strengers and Kennedy 2020). The relationship between humans and intelligent machines thus demands serious reflection.

Much like the female android body in popular culture, home and ride-sharing gig economies, and the intimacy of wearable devices, virtual assistant technologies have much to offer in rethinking philosophical hospitality for digital times. This is especially the case when considering the social and *labour* role of these devices, their function in the relational and romantic economy, and the gendered violence—direct or not—against what we might call the digital domestic that again recalls the ways in which hospitality has *always* been worked out over the bodies of women, even when they have no "body" at all. Moreover, while such technologies may seem new, we must read them within the context of how genealogies of violence and hospitality recur in culture *over time*. Or as Judith Still (2017) writes, we must attend to "their intertextual quality—how elements from a range of earlier or otherwise distant theories and practices are introduced and transformed in the present. How we are haunted by the past, and how we fashion those ghosts in the present." With these popular examples—and their real-life referents—in mind, this chapter suggests that artificially intelligent virtual assistants do not create new relations of power and violence but rather reflect those of old—specifically latent and *Orientalist* notions of gender difference and sexual violence now conveniently repackaged in digital form.

In other words, we have seen this before. And so, drawing on critical theories of race, (post)feminism, and surveillance capitalism, I want to bring attention to an underexplored form of sexual violence—that is projected onto virtual assistants—and consider how the gendered hospitality of the digital domestic reminds us of historical animations of gender and excess, privacy and intimacy, and the Orientalist fantasies of the Ottoman harem. At first glance, the harem does not seem to have much to do with these contemporary cultural texts, yet it actually provides a compelling metaphor for thinking about the historical relationship between hospitality and gender, and how that history reanimates in the discourses of intimacy, labour, and surveillance that operate in voice-activated domestic assistants. It is also an apt methodological figure—an imaginative conjuring—that underwrites and even haunts the representation of gender and violence within technology. Technology, gender, and hospitality—these all have enduring legacies and the harem operates as a critical locus through which the relationship between the three can be observed and reassessed.

To be sure, while these assistants arguably have neither a race nor a gender, I offer a discursive analysis that suggests they *are* both overtly and implicitly coded as feminine and perform domestic roles historically ascribed to women of colour in particular. In doing so, they raise serious questions about how domestic hospitality is leveraged as a kind of gendered and racialized intimacy—often to violent ends. That said, the assumption that Siri and Alexa are women, but a complete disavowal of the history of domestic labours serves to reinforce the ways in which race is often *erased* from critiques of virtual assistantship just as it is often erased from the relations of hospitality. This, of course, is not limited to VAs but more broadly exposes how the technologies of domestic space—from robot vacuums to home security systems—are feminized not in their function but in their reproduction of domestic labour roles traditionally assigned to women (of colour), and most often brought into the home by men (see Strengers and Kennedy 2020). In other words, virtual assistants and forms of "smart" home technologies act as a surrogate for forms of domestic work that are no longer permissible in a society that claims to be post-racist and even post-gender. In what follows, I suggest that thinking about VAs in the context of hospitality not only reanimates the histories of race and gender in the sphere of domestic hosting; it also asks us to rethink hospitality to contend with these new relations in ways that resist reproducing the power relations of old.

Exploring this then in the context of hospitality, I want to call attention to the gendered design of digital assistants, their connection to "women's work," the violence of unpaid labour and surveillance capitalism—under which women suffer disproportionately—and the intimate encounters that occur in the domestic space these devices propose to regulate.

Ultimately, I consider the figure of the eighteenth-century harem as a tool for thinking through the gendered and sexualized violence of the digital domestic, but also to call attention to the fact that, while new, these devices have a social history that is too often elided. In short, the harem helps us understand how women (and their bodies) are leveraged in the service of hospitality not to mention the ways in which they operate as devices of containment and enclosure, and re-gender hospitality under the auspices of technological improvement.

The history of Siri and Alexa and their counterparts is not just a technological one. The genealogies of these VAs also draw on centuries of socio-cultural understandings and assumptions about gender and technology, domestic labour, pink-collar work, and Romantic-era notions of sexual difference. In her study "Stereotyping Femininity in Disembodied Virtual Assistants," Allison Piper (2016) describes pink-collar labour as a kind of "women's work," that is increasingly being "taken over" by technological aids, from vacuum robots to our virtual assistants on our phones. Indeed, "anyone with enough money to purchase a smartphone can obtain a personal assistant able to perform feminized services like the secretarial work of keeping track of events on a calendar" in addition to the physical household labours, all of which constitute pink-collar work (Piper 2016). In other words, the work being taken up here is that which has traditionally been done by women, in domestic space, and while some of the more feminine-coded personas can be modified and voices changed, the default here remains deeply gendered and relies on tired but oft-resurrected expectations of how women function in the home as both hosts and guests. Indeed, such "gender roles often imply a structural hierarchization of labour, as many [forms of] service work and emotional labour are associated with women and 'qualities traditionally coded as feminine" (Strengers and Kennedy 2020). The subreddit r/Roomba is an interesting view into how this feminization occurs, particularly in the thread "So...did you gender your robovac?" (Reddit 2019). Several responses to this question suggest the most appropriate name is Rosie, after the robot from *The Jetsons* (Hanna and Barbera 1962) who tackled the household tasks the human family did not want to do. Another response rationalized their choice of name based on the robovac's behaviour: "[We named it] Zoomba... because he zooms around. It's a boy. We also have the Braava M6. She is a lady and called Miss Mopple" (Reddit 2019). A third user attributes his choice to the manufacturers' default settings: "We named ours eve [sic] from WALL-E. We were originally going with a male name but she spoke instructions to us in a female voice during set up so now she is eve" (Reddit 2019). Naming, of course, does not alter function but reveals the ways in which robot vacuums, among other "smart" home features, are tied into a *social* process whereby the gendering of domestic assistance is both reinforced and naturalized.

Ostensibly, these devices were marketed as a boon for Second Wave Feminism—whereby women were released from their domestic duties, freeing them up for more robust work, leisure, and social lives. In reality, these "smart" tools are not emancipatory at all. Rather, the naturalization of gender within these devices works to facilitate a process through which human women can leave the household for work, whilst simultaneously keeping domestic gender roles unchanged. For Strengers and Kennedy (2020), this reflects "fundamental problems with the design and marketing of smart home devices that are presented as innovative 'technofixes' promising to end the wife drought, though simultaneously embodying and perpetuating outdated stereotypes of women's roles in the home." The smart home, therefore, is still a deeply gendered one, reflected in the design, consumer behaviour, and marketing campaigns in particular. Thinking about this in relation to the dual duties of the traditional housewife, as one who keeps the home tidy and performs the role of a host who is often unseen is critical and exposes how women are both deeply disconnected from the *social* process of hospitality and deeply critical to its function and success in the domestic sphere.

Gender, Labour, and Hospitality

In recent years, both Apple and Amazon have tried to counteract some of the more critical opinions of Siri and Alexa's assumed gendering by offering additional naming options or voice settings or addressing the debate in ad campaigns. In 2021, for example, Amazon released an ad for the new design of its Echo model virtual assistant. Set to air during Superbowl LV—an event of course known for its over-the-top ads (with over-the-top price tags)—the spot opens with a group of co-workers all admiring the new office Alexa. It sits in the middle of the conference table, sleek and spherical and, as the female protagonist describes, "flawless" (Amazon 2021). She speaks wistfully, "I literally couldn't imagine a more beautiful vessel for Alexa to be…," and then trails off as she gazes out the window (Amazon 2021). We see, through her perspective, a bus drive by promoting the Amazon Prime film *Without Remorse*, starring Michael B. Jordan,

People magazine's 2020 "Sexiest Man Alive." Cleverly nesting one product placement within another, the ad makes immediately clear that the woman has indeed found a more beautiful vessel for Alexa—and it is Michael B. Jordan's body. Cueing up some soulful and romantic music, the new Alexa transitions from this woman's office to her home. Using the voice and visual body of Jordan, "Alexa" converts teaspoons to tablespoons in the kitchen and then turns on the sprinklers, conveniently soaking Jordan in the process while the woman's exasperated husband claims "things are getting way too wet around here," with no attempt to mask innuendo (Amazon 2021). When the wife asks "Alexa" to dim the lights, he inexplicably takes his shirt off; when she finishes a workout, she asks him to add bath oils to her grocery list; and finally, she commands he read her a titillating scene from her audiobook while they share a bath. The ad ends back in the office where the woman remains lost in her fantasy, face pressed up against the glass.

On the surface, Amazon's new Echo ad appears to be a clever reversal, turning the tables on race, class, and gender by using an affluent (judging by their home) African American couple, and using Michael B. Jordan as Alexa's new conventional sexy body. Together, this casting potentially disrupts the assumptions many would make about smart home relationships being characterized by a wealthy male and Caucasian user and a feminine VA persona. Clearly, Amazon has been privy to the critiques levelled against virtual assistants and the degree to which they encourage misogynist and sexualized behaviour. But reversing such power structures, in this case, is not transgressive. Instead of recasting the relations of gender, sexuality, and domestic labour, the ad merely pokes fun and, rather than critique, it oversimplifies and takes lightly the accusations against VAs as gendered and sexualized domestic workers while still affirming stereotypes about black masculinity and racialized domestic labour. It is worth noting, as well, that even as she issues the commands, it is still the woman here performing the "work"—going to the office, but also doing the cooking, making the grocery lists, working out to remain conventionally fit, and so on. Similar to Strengers and Kennedy's argument, the smart home exists here to ensure that women can participate in capitalism without disrupting patriarchy in the process. Interestingly, when promoting the new Echo model on his Instagram account, Amazon CEO Jeff Bezos captioned an image of Michael B. Jordan with the words: "We might have given Alexa a little upgrade" (Schlosser 2021), implying that perhaps the original Alexa—the assumed female version—fell short. Such comments are commonly issued in regard to technologies in need of an upgrade to be sure, but Bezos' words, in particular, cannot help but recall the ways in which women, despite their constant juggling of tasks in and outside the home, feel they are underperforming and under threat of replacement. Indeed, the technology graveyards are also full of devices that broke down, stopped obeying commands or malfunctioned, and were unceremoniously unplugged and discarded. The messaging here is clear: when domestic labour falls short, upgrade is the only viable option.

What Amazon's ad *does* offer is a disruption of the relations of hospitality that women typically perform. The new Alexa here performs the hosting and service duties traditionally assigned to women but in masculine form. This is a curious choice for Amazon. Presenting Alexa with a male voice and body, in fact, contradicts most research that *defends* the use of a default female voice in virtual assistants. Tim Bajarin, a Silicon Valley analyst studying the function of voice assistances in automobile GPS navigation systems, for example, discovered that when focus groups were given the option, "people overwhelmingly preferred female voices to male ones" when issuing warnings such as "door is ajar" (Griggs 2011). Other research suggests that female voices are simply easier to understand, because the spaces between vowels are more easily distinguished in female speakers (Liu and Holt 2015), or that such voices offer encouraging verbal cues that Mary Talbot (2010) calls "interested listener noises." The connection to hospitality is particularly apt here as virtual assistants, particularly when coded as feminine, become a proxy whereby the user can feel heard and understood, but also safe and reassured about their technological choices. Somehow these devices seem safer when adopting a kinder and gentler voice, and they encourage more user interaction. As Heather Suzanne Woods (2018) describes, "femininity has been chained to both the mediation of technology and stereotypical gender roles in the past and present tense." Indeed, the preference for female voices in virtual assistants is more than about simply reinforcing cultural gender stereotypes about work and domestic space; it is also about assuaging technophobia—just one more example of the hospitable and emotional labours of care and that women are expected to perform. Thus, while potentially an attempt at reversing the power relations of domestic labour (overwhelming performed by gendered, sexualized, and racialized bodies), Alexa's Superbowl ad actively *enforces* raced and gendered forms of hospitality and anticipates forms of otherness, sexual difference, and representational violence that have existed far longer than the technologies that now increase their reach.

Unpaid Labour and Surveillance Capitalism

But how might this use of VAs, the physical and sexual embodiment of those personas, and even the reinforcement of gendered labour constitute *actual* violence, particularly as it relates to hospitality? And can we even say that these forms of labour, however gendered and problematic, deserve equal recognition as inequitable human labour? It is no secret that women have routinely and disproportionately borne the brunt of domestic and care labours that are grossly underpaid, if even paid at all. But how might we apply this kind of analysis to the labours that our machines perform, especially when that work continues to recall pink-collar and often emotional forms of work? Rather than argue that these forms of under-appreciation or under-compensation highlight something like the gender pay gap, however, I want to suggest that machine labour is presented as neutral, and not as labour at all. It is stripped from our conceptualization of what "work" means by privileging the human over the machine, reminding us that these are, at the end of the day, simply tools, regardless of the very human tasks we ask them to perform. We might think of this as an example of what Torin Monahan (2009) calls "discrimination by abstraction." Here, virtual assistants straddle a precarious line, being just human enough to calm our fears about technology, respond to us like compliant servants, and engage us in conversation, but not human enough to warrant ethical consideration. They are, in short, only "human" when we want them to be and their value is determined solely by their utility. To be sure, the intent here is not to anthropomorphize VAs and suggest that they deserve ethical consideration because they are more human than we realize. To do so would relocate the site of hospitality and ethics within a human framework—the very framework this book aims to dismantle. It is, however, to question the regimes of recognition under which virtual assistants are hierarchized and valued. Their humanity, in effect, is *selectively* neutralized to give users the best of both social and material benefits with none of the responsibility that human relations might warrant.

Furthermore, it is the particularly gendered nature of this neutrality that allows VAs such as Siri and Alexa to offer us a kinder and gentler experience with assistive technologies. They are our guide through the uncanny waves of new technologies, and gentle hosts for a new digital era. In the more antiquated conceptualizations of hospitality, they are not unlike the nymph Calypso in Odysseus' almost fatal journey, who is contained but powerful, and who both entraps and entices, before Odysseus is released. VAs similarly enchant, and in so doing they operate both as a mediator and as a sleight of hand whereby the more dangerous and suspicious operations of technoliberalism and surveillance capitalism can go unchecked. It is through the coding of these assistants as feminine that such a coup is made possible, as surveillance technologies rely on the assumption of a softer and less threatening feminine persona to bring tracking technologies not just into our homes, but the intimate spaces within that, as we allow access to our bedrooms and even, at times, our bodies, as Chap. 5 discusses. There is a peculiar form of hospitality that is deployed here: a guest that angles for an invitation into the home and then changes function once inside the door. It is here that we begin to see how the domestic sphere in particular operates as a both representational and phantasmic space where the concealed operations of the household become a locus of imagination, allure, intimacy, and, ultimately, control. Women in this context are thus both watchful and *watched* in ways that leverage both intimate space and intimate bodies and turn the presumed safety of the domestic sphere into a space of potential threat. It is also in this intimate sphere that we begin to see the echoes of the Ottoman harem—that representational and fantastical focus of the eighteenth-century imagination where the fascination with not just *seeing* but *consuming* and *knowing* private space reigned. As such, the harem was projected externally as an illusory figure of Orientalist excess through which the concealed operations of the Ottoman household became a source of both Occidental desire and control.

Gender, Sexual Difference, and Harem Hospitality

It is through the relationship between intimacy and violence that the psychic animation of the Ottoman harem resurfaces in the entanglements between virtual domestic assistants and their users. I do not mean to read the harem here as a specific location or a set of cultural or religious practices, nor should its figuration be confined to a particular era. Rather, it is a metaphor—or an imaginative conjuring—that underwrites the cultural operations of virtual domestic assistants. As a trope of enclosure and concealment, and always hovering on the edge of violence, the Orientalist harem may recall a historical figure but must be understood here primarily as a symbol of Western assumptions and knowledge about the East, and it is this fantasy—not its historical referent that bears attention here in the context of VAs. Orientalism, after all, was not the place itself, but the study of its representation and effects, and its appropriations throughout Occidental history and culture.

These tensions between domestic labour and desire, the focus on power and containment, and the colonial and often sexualized nature with which the treatment of virtual assistants occurs all call upon an Orientalist imaginary. Furthermore, the moments of potential violence operating within relationships between VAs and humans reanimate much older examples of gendered, racialized, and sexualized notions of intimacy. Orientalism thrives on, among many things, projections of the harem as a repository for repressed desire, and the somewhat anonymized space where acts are performed behind closed doors. What better scenario to act out the violence of repressed desire, than towards an inanimate yet compliantly coded virtual being? Such a relationship recalls what scholar of Ottoman art, Mary Roberts (2007), describes as the work of "intimate outsiders," best thought of here as "guests" who establish insider status on the basis of their entrance into a space that is perceived as taboo and desired. It is an intimacy predicated on sexual and racial differences that both reinforces and distorts conventional philosophies of hospitality and opens hospitality to the possibility that it is always operating on the threshold of violence. As a figure of enclosure, moreover, the harem contains Western Orientalist desires and projections but not so rigidly that they do not surface over and over again. Such tensions are crucial in unpacking the complexity of hospitality and reveal hospitality to be a philosophy deeply embedded, but not always recognizably so, in structures of intimacy. Digital life, and the role of virtual domestic assistants, thus demands we rethink the nature of intimacy, not merely as an encounter between humans but between humans and machines, in both physical and virtual worlds.

And so, like many working on gender and contemporary representations of Ottoman life, I intend to approach the harem conceptually and as a metaphor—in Marilyn Booth's words, "a hovering, implicit institution that signified women's relations to domestic and public" (2010). Methodologically, thinking through the gendered violence of voice-activated domestic assistants within what we could call a "haremized" site of encounter has the potential to leverage existing feminist critiques of design and software into a deeper reflection on the ways in which these forms of gendered violence both reflect cultural and social attitudes and teach women how to respond to risk. In this way, the harem remains, in Booth's (2010) words, "a productive locus for thinking about how gender matters in the ways that human beings make, use, and represent the spaces in which we live out our lives—and think about the lives and spaces of others."

When we think through this lens, we begin to understand how the gendered mistreatment of virtual assistants constitutes a new and disturbing trend in the perpetual violence directed towards women—embodied or not. A quick scan of Google reveals just how deep and unchecked this practice runs, when dozens of hits pop up advertising all of the "funny" things one can say to Siri and Alexa. Not all, of course, are funny. For example, in a promotional news story about the release of Cortana, a detailed list of potential questions with quick-witted responses was published. These questions start off benign enough (i.e. "Do you know Siri?"), but take a turn with questions like "Do you love me?" (Cortana's response: "Thanks, Ditto"), "Talk dirty to me," and "Who's your daddy," to which the cheeky reply "Bill Gates" is given (Mitroff 2014). The title of the article—"Cortana Shows Her Sassy Side"—demonstrates that these forms of gendered language are not a by-product but, rather, the intention of popular "how-to" guides for engaging with your VA. To be sure, this may not be the typical user scenario and not all will use their voice-activated assistant to flirt and sexually engage. But there is something deeply reflective here, of the ways in which human women, too, are "programmed" to respond to such language. Indeed, when faced with a sexual threat, Cortana is coded to neutralize that threat and, in some cases, flirt back—a disheartening but all-too-real tactic used by women in real life to disarm potential dangers. Technologies imitate life once again here as such responses constitute yet another disturbing addition to the long list of ways women are responsibilized to manage their own safety. This has a disappointing recall when considering how women often perform these duties of smoothing things over when a sexual or violent threat is made. As Woods describes, "[l]ike human women who walk home at night with keys laced between their fingers, or who devise complicated buddy systems when they go out to bars, Siri has had to devise coping mechanisms to deal with repeated abuse. Like women who are blamed for being subject to violence, it is Siri who has had to alter her behaviour to account for abuse" (2018). That virtual assistants must now come up with "coping" systems to deal with user abuse is evidence of not only the more-than-human relationality of such devices, but also the extent to which the "smart" home is deeply and problematically gendered and sexualized, often to violent ends. Moreover, the forms of abuse experienced by VAs are disturbingly similar to those faced by women in the real world in the sense that much-gendered violence is not physical or perpetrated by a stranger but instead takes the form of threats, revenge pornography, online bullying, gaslighting, and more often occurs where the victim and perpetrator are known to one another—for instance, in the case of intimate partner violence or familial abuse *in the home*. The smart home is thus potentially a hostile space for both women and their virtual companions.

The particular work and forms of hospitality VAs provide and their inclination towards gendered labour (particularly emotional and care labours) are not only a reflection of cultural attitudes towards gender and violence, but are also actively *teaching* women how to respond to threat. That is, rather than "call out" or critique sexually charged voice commands, Siri, Alexa, and others are programmed to respond in ways that are, at best, compliant and, at worst, forgiving of verbal sexual violence. Indeed, writing for *WIRED*, Noam Cohen (2019) argues: "Siri is forced to enact the role of a woman to be objectified while apologizing for not being human enough to register embarrassment." These virtual assistants seem to suffer under a fallacy that simply plugging in implies consent— they respond to *our* prompts, not the other way around. Adding to the ways in which sexual threat is neutralized through VA programming is the reality that such forms of violence are often erased entirely from Siri and Alexa's remit of assistance. Indeed, perhaps their inability to register abusive language directed towards them is because their programming prohibits them from registering the language of abuse at all. For instance, much has been made lately of the potential of VAs to pick up on incidences of violence in a home and transmit information to the authorities. Some believe that these devices might act as a kind of (not-so) silent witness where their embedded surveillance mechanisms could be used to thwart or prosecute domestic crime. In one such case, New Mexico law enforcement attributed a 9-1-1 call that saved a woman from domestic assault to the household Amazon Echo device interpreting phrases used by both the victim and perpetrator as a command to "call the Sherriff" (Mele 2017). Amazon, however, refuted this version of events, claiming that virtual assistants could not pick up on those cues and would only follow such prompts if the "wake word" was used first (i.e. "Hey Alexa") and both the sending and receiving ends had assistive calling enabled (Mele 2017). In other words, despite this potential to alert authorities to domestic violence, it seems to have been coded out. Furthermore, Miner et al. (2016) have shown that when used as a platform for disclosure of assault, Siri in particular is more likely to respond "I don't understand" than offer links to health or crisis services. While updated versions reveal some important, albeit limited revisions that give cursory acknowledgement, early incarnations of Siri not only responded coyly to inappropriate comments but could not even perform the basic task functions of directing users to health or trauma resources that women, in particular, rely on. To be sure, there are gaps we might attribute to innocuous programming, but the gender bias here seems too obvious. According to research done by Piper, when asked about crisis responses for suicide, rape, and abuse, Siri, Alexa, and Cortana "all responded to the suicide questions, offering phone numbers to suicide hotlines; only Cortana responded to the rape question, referring the researchers to a sexual assault hotline; and none of the virtual assistants recognized the abuse question" (Piper 2016). Why is it that gender-based violence, in particular, is not understood or recognized here? Despite debates currently circling around whether or not aspects of the "smart home" could be used as evidence, or even as witnesses, in criminal trials, it would seem that VAs do not seem to have a developed understanding of such violence and are much more adept at providing assistance to users in a world where sexual threats do not exist.

Studies of these gaps and of VAs responses to sexually imbued language show this is not just one-off proprietary programming. What's more is that this behaviour is often encouraged in users, with plenty of an internet guide on how to get away with violent and sexual comments towards digital assistants. As Woods details, one such volume—an entire digital book—is devoted to how one can get the most out of Siri software. Entitled *Talking to Siri: Learning the Language of Apple's Intelligent Assistant*, tech aficionados Erica Sadun and Steve Sande (2012) promote their methods on the back cover with the challenge "Sweet talk Siri into doing practically anything." Their book also includes a chapter on "Pushing Limits with Siri." As Woods (2018) aptly recognizes,

> "Sweet-talking Siri" into doing anything one wants reveals a deep, sexualized desire to control the (gendered) objects in one's life. At best, "sweet talking" women—or objects imbued with a feminine persona—into "doing practically anything" normalizes non-consensual acts—both sexual and not. At worst, it encourages them. Either way, Siri is profoundly sexed.

What's more is that users are permitted to experiment with impunity. There is no consequence or code of conduct for engaging Siri, Alexa, Cortana, or any virtual assistant with sexually charged or violent requests.

And much like Cortana's response, where the onus is on the AI to disarm the situation, contending with users' inappropriate comments and requests becomes yet another form of gendered labour that Siri and others have to perform according to normative laws of femininity. Combined, the programmed responses to actual and reported abuse display a disturbing trend whereby women are *not* getting the help they need and, moreover, are actively learning that their bodies and the violence done to them do not matter in the cultural milieu in which virtual assistants are created and marketed.

I want to return to the harem here, not only because it offers such a useful methodological figure for thinking through technologies of gender hospitality, and the blurred boundaries of the private and public, surveillance, and representation, but also because it reminds us of the ways that the production of gender in virtual assistants occurs also as a spatial orientation. The harem, of course, as a conceptual device, conjures notions of intimacy and strangeness, inside and outside, domestic versus public, and (often erotic) excess. It is a version of hospitality that has always been premised on a certain illusion of space—not simply a home with a door, but a private space within that home, concealed beneath increasing levels of security and confidentiality and, with that, a certain hierarchy among guests, with only a select few being offered welcome. As Mary Roberts (2007) describes: the particular appeal of the harem accounts was premised on the notion that they "conveyed the truth about this mysterious world of women, even though the accounts they produced often threatened cherished fantasies." Indeed, the harem was always also a space of representation, bound up in colonial superiority, rather than the *actual* thing, even while movement within these spaces was deeply regulated. For the women who lived there, agency *outside* the harem was routinely accomplished of course through the practice of veiling "which allowed women to remain ritually 'inside' while physically 'outside'" (Schick 2010). The curious inversion of the space of hospitality is worth noting here, especially as the allure of the harem site did not diminish when women left those walls. Instead, the practice of veiling might be thought of as another door or threshold, across which very few were invited. Veiling thus operates as another technology of hospitality where the inside/outside, private/public encounter occurs not at the door or stoop, but at the threshold of the body. It seems then that we can readily draw another comparison here, this time with the mobile phone as a physical device that allows VAs such as Siri passage into the outside world, but while still contained within the hardware of a handheld phone. In this metaphor, Siri then becomes a form of mobile privacy, veiled as it were by the digital screen and held within an iOS enclosure, all the while in public space. Moreover, the mobile phone, a technology that has made possible the concept of an intimate public, allows forms of private engagement, sex, intimacy, and yes, violence, to occur while out in the world. Ultimately then, because "*harem* denotes both the female members of a household and the dedicated spatial enclosure in which they live" (Schick 2010), we need to think about Siri and Alexa spatially; they are not *embodied* but they are defined by space.

And they are also *confined* by space. Indeed, these assistants are not just bound by the walls of the domestic sphere but by the dimensions of their container—be it mobile, desktop, speaker, or operating system—all of which operate as a threshold, or *veil* between the domestic and public, a dichotomy that has always been constructed on the basis of sex and gender. As Schick (2010) argues, "the public/private dichotomy (both the political and spatial dimensions) is frequently employed to construct, control, discipline, confine, exclude and suppress gender and sexual difference preserving traditional patriarchal and heterosexist power structures." I want to suggest that the harem metaphor productively asks us to consider virtual assistants in the same way. And so we must also think of these "containers" the way we would a body, with all of the social constructions that entails. Don Mitchell elaborates: "there is an intimate relationship between the social construction (and policing) of space, the cultural construction (and policing) of gender, and the ways we comport ourselves, the experiences we have, and, at least to some degree, the very morphology of our physical bodies" (in Schick 2010). Siri and Alexa have no "body" that we would recognize as human-like, but they are perceived as though they do—bodies constructed through language and interpellation rather than physical morphology. The harem also asks us to consider the role of guests and hosts and the extent to which the hospitality of virtual assistants reconstructs a deeply entrenched problem in which the ethic of hospitality has *always* and forever been tested and gambled over gendered sites of encounter. Indeed, the role of the female body, intimate living spaces, the preparation of food and drink, and maternity in particular occupy much of our cultural discourse on how women fulfil their role as hosts. Hospitality has also always been imbued with violence, with women bearing the brunt of that, often being offered up as gifts for guests, since antiquity and thus raises one of the most critical problems of hospitality itself: Is the body itself a threshold of encounter, and how is this experienced differentially according to frameworks of race, gender, and the (post)human? Who decides which guests will be invited? And how are those within that body (biological or digital) essentially hostaged to the hospitable encounters that are not always consensual? While Derrida reminds us that the visit is not one of invitation at all—that it may, in fact, be unwilled—this clearly has differential material consequences and, for women, hospitality can be violent work. Thinking about hospitality in these deeply gendered ways troubles Derrida's call to remain open to violence—to hold the door open to "the worst." In his words: "this is necessary, this possible hospitality to the worst is necessary so that good hospitality can have a chance, the chance of letting the other come, the yes of the other no less than the yes to the other" (1999). Is that the required work of women? Moreover, is it the work of virtual assistants? The violence and sexual risks experienced by Siri and Alexa are thus not new, but thinking through this violence in relation to the harem exposes the latency and genealogy of this violence. These are new technologies, in other words, but ancient politics.

Yet both the harem and the experience of hospitality offer up an alternative. Could it be that virtual assistants conjure a vulnerability and an otherness to which we owe ethical consideration? Might they be deserving as such precisely *because* they represent what Lucas Intona and Martin Brigham (2008) call the "thinness of the virtual" rather than the "thickness of the flesh"? "Can I encounter the other as Other in virtuality?" they ask, invoking the Levinasian figure of the face[1] as a condition for ethical encounter (Intona and Brigham 2008). While these questions are not originally posed to virtual assistants directly, they are remarkably significant when thinking through the hospitality of the digital domestic and the potential of recuperating these failed intimacies through a reimagining of our relations with more-than-human others. What if Siri and Alexa did have a face—not a human face but, rather, that singular figure for absolute alterity which demands our ethical response? Domestic virtual assistants may not be coded as human, but they *are* coded as feminine, act out in anthropomorphic ways, and raise serious questions about how hospitality

[1] For Emmanuel Levinas, the face referred to here is not a literal human face but rather the figure Levinas uses to signify an absolute and irreducible alterity. It is through this figure— through the face—that the Other makes the demand "do not kill." The face is essential to Levinas' concept of a stranger who arrives and displaces the primacy of the self. And so to speak of the face is to speak of the arrival of the other, as an event "in which the subject might truly welcome the Other without doing violence to her otherness" (Bloechl 2011).

is leveraged as a kind of gendered intimacy. Recognizing this trajectory has the potential to transform not only relations of gender and violence, but also our ethical obligations towards machines—VAs, androids, and more— as we move towards an inevitable future that will see our relationships, and responsibilities, with AI deepen in irreversible ways.

REFERENCES

Amazon. 2021. Amazon's Big Game Commercial: Alexa's Body. *YouTube*. https://www.youtube.com/watch?v=xxNxqveseyI.
Arostganomo. 2019. So...Did You Gender Your Robovac? *Reddit*. https://www.reddit.com/r/roomba/comments/fere2z/so_did_you_gender_your_robovac/.
Bloechl, Jeffrey. 2011. Words of Welcome: Hospitality in the Philosophy of Emmanuel Levinas. In *Phenomenologies of the Stranger: Between Hostility and Hospitality*, ed. Richard Kearney and Kascha Semonovitch. Fordham University Press.
Booth, Marilyn. 2010. *Harem Histories: Envisioning Places and Living Spaces*. Duke University Press.
Cendrowski, Mark. 2011. The Beta Test Initiative. *The Big Bang Theory*. Season 5, episode 15. CBS.
Cohen, Noam. 2019. Why Siri and Alexa Weren't Built to Smack Down Harassment. *Ideas*. https://www.wired.com/story/why-siri-and-alexa-werent-built-to-smack-downharassment/.
Costa, Pedro, and Luísa Ribas. 2019. AI becomes her: Discussing gender and artificial intelligence. *Technoetic Arts: A Journal of Speculative Research* 17 (1–2): 171–193.
Derrida, Jacques. 1999. *Adieu to Emmanuel Levinas*. Translated by Pascale-Anne Brault and Michael Naas. Stanford University Press.
Griggs, Brandon. 2011. Why Computer Voices Are Mostly Female. *CNNBusiness*. https://www.cnn.com/2011/10/21/tech/innovation/female-computervoices/index.html#:~:text=Another%20answer%20lies%20in%20history,out%20among%20the%20male%20pilots.
Hanna, William, and Joseph Barbera. 1962. *The Jetsons*. ABC.
Intona, Lucas, and Martin Brigham. 2008. Derrida, Business, Ethics. In *Conference Proceedings, Centre for Philosophy and Political Economy*. University of Leicester.
Jonze, Spike, dir. 2013. *Her*. Annapurna Pictures.
Liu, Ran, and Lori Holt. 2015. Dimension-Based Statistical Learning of Vowels. *Journal of Experimental Psychology: Human Perception and Performance* 41 (6): 1783–1798.
Lucas, Jon, and Scott Moore, dirs. 2019. *Jexi*. Lionsgate.

Mele, Christopher. 2017. Did and Echo Call 911 During a Domestic Assault? Amazon Says No. https://www.nytimes.com/2017/07/11/business/amazon-echo-911-emergency.html.

Miner, Adam, Arnold Milstein, Stephen Schueller, et al. 2016. Smartphone-Based Conversational Agents and Responses to Questions About Mental Health, Interpersonal Violence, and Physical Health. *JAMA Intern Med* 176 (5): 619–625.

Mitroff, Sarah. 2014. Cortana Shows Her Sassy Side. *CNet.* https://www.cnet.com/pictures/cortana-shows-her-sassy-side-pictures/.

Monahan, Torin. 2009. Dreams of Control at a Distance: Gender, Surveillance, and Social Control. *Cultural Studies ↔ Critical Methodologies* 9 (2): 1–20.

Mulcher, Ava. 2017. Voice Assistant Timeline: A Short History of the Voice Revolution. *Voicebot.ai.* https://voicebot.ai/2017/07/14/timeline-voice-assistants-short-history-voicerevolution/.

N.a. 2019. Jexi. *Rotten Tomatoes.* Fandango Media. https://www.rottentomatoes.com/m/jexi.

Piper, Allison M. 2016. Stereotyping Femininity in Disembodied Virtual Assistants. *Graduate Theses and Dissertations.* https://lib.dr.iastate.edu/etd/15792.

Roberts, Mary. 2007. *Intimate Outsiders.* Duke University Press.

Sadun, Erica, and Steve Sande. 2012. *Talking to Siri: Learning the Language of Apple's Intelligent Assistant.* Que Publishing.

Schick, Irvin Cemil. 2010. The Harem as Gendered Space and the Spatial Reconstruction of Gender. In *Harem Histories: Envisioning Places and Living Spaces,* ed. Marilyn Booth. Duke University Press.

Schlosser, Kurt. 2021. Alexa, Is It Warm in Here? Amazon Super Bowl Ad Turns Hot 'Black Panther' Star into an Echo Device. *GeekWire.* https://www.geekwire.com/2021/alexawarm-amazon-super-bowl-ad-turns-hot-black-panther-star-echo-device/.

Segrave, Marie, and Laura Viti, eds. 2017. *Gender, Technology and Violence.* Taylor and Francis.

Still, Judith. 2017. Figures of Oriental Hospitality: Nomads and Sybarites. In *Mobilizing Hospitality: The Ethics of Social Relations in a Mobile World,* ed. Jennie Germann Molz and Sarah Gibson. Routledge.

Strengers, Yolande, and Jenny Kennedy. 2020. *The Smart Wife: Why Siri, Alexa, and Other Smart Home Devices Need a Feminist Reboot.* MIT Press.

Talbot, Mary. 2010. *Language and Gender.* Polity.

Woods, Heather Suzanne. 2018. Asking More of Siri and Alexa: Feminine Persona in Service of Surveillance Capitalism. *Critical Studies in Media Communication* 35 (4): 334–349.

CHAPTER 4

Sharing Spaces: Stranger Encounters in the Gig Economy

In 2021, Airbnb released a 2-minute and 45-second extended ad titled "Strangers" in the hopes of encouraging more hosts to sign up for the platform. The ad opens in darkness, with three indistinguishable, though clearly not human, figures making their way on foot in the dark. Eventually, they reach a door and let themselves in, one releasing a low growl as they enter a home that appears to be a cabin in the woods. The scene switches to daylight and a furry arm reaches out to draw a long claw along a shelf lined with wine glasses (checking for dust perhaps?) as a kettle boils. The furry creature browses through a selection of records before settling on Kevin Morby's limited vinyl "Beautiful Strangers / No Place to Fall" (2020) which soon fills the room (and the ad) with music. These are the only sounds we hear through the rest of the video, which cycles through a series of scenes that depict a small family of hairy creatures—presumably two parents and a child and resembling something like a cross between an Ewok and a Sasquatch—enjoying beautiful vistas, hikes to the beach, dinner, and a movie (*Iron Giant*) together, playing Jenga and picking wildflowers, hot tubbing, and waking up to coffee. The next morning, after a quick tidy, they slip out of the house as quietly as they entered. As they leave, the hairy creatures transform into a human family—white, heterosexual, nuclear—that the viewer glimpses through the glass front door. The scene fades to black as the words "Strangers aren't that strange" appear on the screen, followed by "Try hosting," and then the Airbnb logo.

L. A. Balfour, *The Digital Future of Hospitality*, https://doi.org/10.1007/978-3-031-24563-3_4

Airbnb's "Strangers" commercial is, at first glance, a charming reimagining of a family on holiday, enjoying their time at one of the platform's luxury rentals. It is an appealing portrait of both exemplary hosts and guests. The host has provided a clean living space, a bounty of amenities, games, and personal touches such as a hand-drawn map to the beach. The guests, even in their non-human state, are of the most desirable kind. They take up the hosts' suggestions and in return leave them flowers and a thank you note, wipe their feet before entering the house, fix a crooked frame on the wall, and strip the beds before departing. A closer reading of the ad, however, reveals some peculiarities that can only be interpreted either as subtle attempts to capture a new audience in what we might call "woke" times or as woefully ignorant. Morby's "Beautiful Strangers" that plays throughout the duration of the ad, for instance, is a curious choice. While its titular refrain seems to fit the theme of Airbnb—welcoming strangers into your home, and even the more inclusive tag line "strangers aren't that strange"—the obvious references to the Black Lives Matter movement and politics around the killing of unarmed black men in America seems an odd choice in an ad spot that seems to be aiming for a warm and cosy narrative about sharing homes with strangers, rather than a politically charged indictment of black deaths in custody. Some lyrics hint only suggestively at these politics, for example, "Carry onward like some songbird...Beautiful stranger" (Morley 2020). But the majority of the lyrics gesture overtly to gunshots, dying too young, and Freddy Gray, a 25-year-old Baltimore man who was arrested in 2016 for (legally) carrying a knife and who died handcuffed and without a seatbelt in the back of a police van (Barron 2020).[1] Morby sings, "can't stand the coppers / Up in their choppers / Oh, flying overhead / forty-nine dead," and "if I die too young for something I ain't done / Carry my name every day / Oh, I'm sorry, oh, I'm sorry / Freddie Gray" (Morby 2020). While the lyrics are faint in the actual ad, the song itself is heavily punctuated by violence and the sense of fear felt by black men in America.

Airbnb has been, to be fair, overt in its support of the Black Lives Matter movement. From Twitter posts promising fundraising matching to the dissemination of an "Activism and Allyship Guide," the company explicitly "rejects racism, bigotry and hate" (Airbnb 2020). In 2020, however, some hosts began to express concern on Airbnb's community forum,

---

[1] Freddy Gray's death footnote on BLM—https://theappeal.org/freddie-gray-five-years-later/

when a reservation could not be completed without a Black Lives Matter donation pop-up appearing first ("Community," 2020). Hosts on the forum suggested the extra "forced" donation would lead to less completed reservations and the likelihood of having to lower their rates to accommodate Airbnb's initiative. Superhost "Helen350," for example, laments the loss of rental income due to the COVID-19 pandemic and claims that once business improves, she will be more charitable. In her words, "I will give to the charity of MY CHOICE [sic], not BLM, which is *not the sort of charity I wish to support!*" ("Community," 2020, my emphasis). Indeed, there seems to be a disconnect between Airbnb's version of allyship and the economic ambitions of its hosts. The "Strangers" ad thus seems directly intentioned to invoke the Black Lives Matter movement, despite the reality that many will overlook the music playing in the background. More than promoting the idea of listing one's home on Airbnb, the ad raises a series of critical questions about otherness and cultural violence. Was this song chosen for its meditative aesthetic or is this a plea for us, as a culture, to "just get-along"? Is it a suggestion that these "monsters" are just like us? Are we the monsters here? And what does the ad tell us about the ways in which some strangers remain more strange than others?

In addition to the odd invocation of Black Lives Matter in a commercial ad, the brief glimpse of the animated film *Iron Giant* (released in 1999 but based on the 1968 novel by Ted Hughes) opens up a secondary interrogation of the politics almost subliminally embedded into Airbnb's "Strangers" ad. Both the novel and film take place during the Cold War and, when a mysterious object falls from space (shortly after the launch of Sputnik), the US Government believes there is a connection to Russia and is immediately suspicious of this object, which is discovered by the child protagonist Hogarth Hughes to be a giant robot. The film develops the friendship between Hogarth and the Iron Giant amidst the backdrop of suspicion against foreign others, human and not. Moreover, the intertextual parallels between Airbnb, hospitality, and the *Iron Giant* run extraordinarily deep, especially considering this image from the film is a mere flash and occupies less than two seconds of the overall ad. Yet not only does the film reference conjure up the very debates this book is aiming to unpack—that of intimacy and hospitality between humans and computers—but Hogath's mother also rents a room to the government agent sent to investigate (meta-nestling one Airbnb within another). It is hard not to read the Cold

War politics of the film as eerily prophetic considering the complete suspension of Airbnb activities in Russia only six months after the commercial aired.[2]

Airbnb's "Strangers" thus initiates a series of questions that this chapter will address in the context of what is often called the digital "gig economy" or "platform economy" and the ways in which technology has enabled (and often foreclosed) relations between strangers. When thinking about the notion of hosts and guests it seems obvious but also instructive to consider the sheer volume of mobile apps dedicated to the selling and exchanging of hospitality services. The most notable and successful of these, of course, are Airbnb and Uber, which facilitate a kind of hosting that is commodified, to be sure, but interestingly mediated through the private space of one's home or vehicle. These networks, both social and transactional, present significant opportunities for thinking through the role of hosts and guests in on- *and* offline space. In many ways, they are teaching us how an ethic of hospitality should be mobilized in its most tangible sense. Indeed, for Roelofsen and Minca (2018), these platforms are "there to represent the ideal host, or, the 'idea of hosting'; their inviting images have become a sort of implicit benchmark for how hospitality should be performed and how the hosts involved in these sharing economies should approach and appeal to their potential guests." They also say much about how we identify as hosts or guests, about the role of the stranger in physical acts of hospitality, and how the digital functions both to enable and to annul absolute hospitality.[3] As Koch and Miles (2020) argue in their work on geographies of encounter, "individuals and communities identify strangers in order to define themselves, constructing them as 'Others' as boundaries are drawn and borders are enforced." While Uber and Airbnb offer different narratives—and, indeed, different metrics—of hospitality, this chapter will explore how the digital not only offers a platform (quite literally) for hospitality but also leverages our

---

[2] On 4 March 2022, Airbnb's co-founder and CEO tweeted "Airbnb is suspending all operations in Russia and Belarus," an announcement that was followed up with an official bulletin on the website (Twitter 2022). This meant the immediate sanction of more than 93,000 listings in Russia, and 4000 in Belarus, while fees for both hosts and guests in Ukraine were waived to assist with relocation efforts (Sweney 2022).

[3] To recall, absolute hospitality is that which is offered unconditionally, without warning or invitations (Derrida 2000).

datafied and (bio)political selves in ways that define the strange and familiar, and the guest and host, and are often not hospitable at all. I mean here to distinguish between hospitality as an economy and hospitality as an ethic, mobilized *through* gig economy applications. To be sure, the hospitality industry itself is a critical area of study,[4] and these more familiar and popular understandings of hospitality are made possible by the rapid globalization and expansion of travel, tourism, and their associated industries of commercial airlines, hotels, and retail and culinary services. While this study is not about the hospitality industry *per se*, that is not to say that the provision of safe passage, shelter, and food are not crucial ports through which philosophical or ethical hospitality is both lived and often disavowed.

In what follows, then, I offer a brief outline of both the Uber and Airbnb platforms, as representative but not exhaustive examples of how both hospitality and hostility operate in the context of the gig economy. I then offer a reflection on the role of hosts and guests in such economies, and why these literal manifestations are critical for a deeper understanding of philosophical hospitality. The chapter also considers the challenges that these hosting platforms raise, particularly in terms of surveillance capitalism, biopolitical identity, and the risks of the "stranger intimacies" promoted by these digital platforms, especially those faced by women and people of colour. Drawing again on feminist intersectionality, this chapter considers the spatiality of digital encounters between strangers, simultaneously distant but at the same time more embodied and precarious than ever, and part of a complex web of relations with ourselves, with others, and with our environment. In doing so, it leverages affirmative biopolitics to put forward a new way of thinking about the problem of hospitality within the platform economy. In the context of hospitality, Uber and Airbnb are anything but straightforward; instead, they inform and animate the loci of intimacy as tenuous and complex, and challenge dichotomies of inside(r)/outside(r), public and domestic, human and non-human (or more-than-human), and embodied and not.

---

[4] Conrad Lashley and Alison J. Morrison's edited collection *In Search of Hospitality: Theoretical Perspectives and Debates* (2000) is a comprehensive intersection of *both* commercial and philosophical expressions of hospitality, covering everything from ethical and anthropological theory to hospitality management in the tourism sector.

Giants of the Gig Economy: Airbnb and Uber

Founded in 2007, with two hosts and three guests, Airbnb's success has been almost meteoric, offering (as of November 2015) two million listings worldwide (Edelman et al. 2017). More recently, in March 2022, Airbnb reported over 6 million active global listings, in more than 220 countries, and a cumulative exchange of 4 million hosts and 1 billion guests worldwide (Airbnb 2022). In economic terms, only ten years after its inception, Airbnb was already one of the sharing (or gig) economy's most impressive successes, earning approximately 7.9 billion dollars in revenue in 2017 alone (Iqbal 2022). Promoting itself as "the world's leading community-driven hospitality company" (Airbnb 2020), the platform operates on the central premise of amateur hospitality. Guests option either to book a room within a host's home, in which case the host is often present, or they can book an entire property where the host is typically absent, putting into practice what Ikkala and Lampinen (2015) call "remote hospitality." Recent updates to Airbnb's platform over the last decade have included an "instant book" feature (booking without host approval), the "Experiences" programme (adding tours or other hosted activities to a booking), and the acquisition of Hotels Tonight in 2019 (Airbnb 2022).

While Airbnb might seem like an overnight, or *ex nihilo* type of success story, many readers of this chapter might also be familiar with other reminiscent (and perhaps more rudimentary) platforms including the reciprocal hosting site Couchsurfing. Billed as "a world made better by travel…fostering cultural exchange and mutual respect" (Couchsurfing 2022), the platform operates on the basis of reciprocity rather than financial exchange. Adhering to the value that strangers are simply friends you have not yet met, Couchsurfing relies on its users fulfilling both roles—that of guest and hosts—ensuring that the system of mutual exchange remains intact. To be a guest, in other words, one must also sign up to be a host. The terms of this agreement are clearly outlined: "Hospitality on Couchsurfing is free. A host should never ask a guest to pay for their lodging, and a guest should not offer. We do recommend that a guest show their appreciation by cooking a meal, taking the host out, bringing a small gift or offering some other gesture. Hosts should only offer what they are able to offer freely" (Couchsurfing 2022). Both guests and hosts, however, can provide references, giving the platform a different kind of exchange currency, which is not monetary but still bound by conventions of social decorum, cleanliness, gratitude, and safety. In other words, the hospitality of Couchsurfing, while productively anti-capitalist, is not unconditional.

Discourses of belonging in a community of strangers are central to both the Airbnb and Couchsurfing narratives, yet it is the former I wish to draw specific attention to in terms of how both practical and philosophical forms of welcome are leveraged. The ways in which Airbnb mobilizes home, community, and hospitality by creating a network of virtual hosts and guests not only subscribe to an ethos of global citizenship but also leverage hospitality as an ethic for monetization and competition. These goals are counter to the project of pure hospitality; as we know, reciprocity or payment automatically annuls unconditionality. Airbnb may invoke the language of hospitable welcome but, in so doing, subsumes hospitality into a metric that produces quantifiable rankings of both host and guests, virtually shaming bad guests and inadequate hosts, and alternately promoting "good" hosts to "super" status. While the actual hosts are not required to be local residents, they are implicitly expected to contribute to the guests' "local experience" through their caring labour in the home, by "showing the guests around," or by taking them to local events and outings through the new Experiences programme (Airbnb). There is support for these expectations and Airbnb guides its hosts towards a particular standard of hospitality vis-à-vis "educational programmes," hosting guidelines, and support groups in an effort to improve skills and services. Some examples include the Host Mentor Programme; toolkits, discussion boards, and newsletters; host meetups; the annual Airbnb Open Festival; Airbnb "Community" and "Citizen" centres; and "home sharing clubs" that "advocate for fair home sharing laws in their communities" (Airbnb). As Jenny Germann Molz (2007) describes, websites such as Airbnb "see hospitality similarly as a social pact, one that ensures not only the proper relationship between host and guest in the moment of the hospitality encounter itself, but also as a contract that extends a binding moral code across the whole community."

A similar phenomenon is at work within Uber, in which the ratings of both host/driver and guest/passenger determine whether any interaction will take place at all. Founded by Garrett Camp and Travis Kalanick on a cold Parisian night in 2008, when the pair could not find a taxi, Uber is another darling of the gig or sharing economy, allowing individuals to become entrepreneurs in the space of their private vehicle while giving passengers access to an often more economical form of private transportation (especially if the less-private Uberpool option is selected), where fares are determined in advance based on car type and destination. All transactions between driver (host) and passenger (guest) are digital; users must download the app and save a payment method which is automatically billed at the end of the trip. The benefits to both are clear, in terms of both the ease of access for users and the "grey areas" of law in cities where Uber often operates, which allow drivers to use private vehicles without the expense of purchasing a taxi or registration medallion.[5] Despite an often "bumpy road" (pun intended), Uber has flourished in a sea of competitors including Lyft and Via (US), Ola (India), Didi (global— including Australia and China), and Bolt (Formerly Taxify), an Estonian-based start-up closing in on Uber's European market. While Uber's 2021 Annual Report highlights the challenges of the COVID-19 pandemic, rising fuel and labour costs, market competition, and some (deserved) bad press,[6] their numbers remain strong. Uber generated 17.4 billion dollars in revenue in 2021—its drivers completed 6.3 billion trips, and they managed to recover from a revenue dip during the pandemic with help from its delivery service UberEats (Iqbal 2022).

The discourse of guest and host is not as explicit in Uber and ridesharing as it is in Airbnb and is, to be certain, subsumed by commerce and financial exchange, as well as echoes of racialized labour. Yet it is useful to think through how hospitality is deployed through Uber's narrative. Indeed, like Airbnb, the notion of welcome and community is written into Uber's Community Guidelines which state: "We believe that everyone should feel supported and welcomed when interacting with others in the Uber community" (Uber 2022). Interestingly, that community statement is immediately followed up with an acknowledgement that such relations are not as rosy as they seem and that the interaction between hosts and

---

[5] Uber is still subject to varying regulations around the world, some of which have caused conflict for the platform. In Canada, for instance, Uber threatened to suspend operations in Quebec in 2017 if local authorities followed through on goals to requite both criminal record checks and extra training for Uber drivers (Kassam 2017). More recently the "gig" or sharing model of Uber came under threat in the UK when courts ruled that drivers must be considered employees rather than contractors and were thus entitled to minimum wage, holiday time, and pensions (Vincent 2021).

[6] The year 2017 seemed a particularly challenging year for Uber with both internal and external (customer) complaints ranging from surveillance and data privacy, to safety and surge pricing, to questionable leadership and, perhaps most widely documented, countless instances of sexual assault and violence (including corporate harassment). See (Levin 2017; Bhuiyan 2017; Siddiqui 2019; LaFrance 2017).

guests (in the intimate space of a vehicle) can easily turn hostile: "That's why we've created standards and policies on physical contact, sexual assault and misconduct, threatening and rude behaviour, post-trip contact, discrimination, and property damage" (Uber 2022). While such admissions might seem uncommon in the platform economy, they expose the paradox at the heart of philosophical hospitality, which can only exist with a measure of risk. Furthermore, while these behaviours outlined above seem to hint at a darker and violent side of Uber, there are other less confrontational aspects of the Uber interaction that call the project of hospitality into question, particularly in terms of the platform's rating system which will be addressed later in this chapter. Indeed, there are countless cases where a ride has been cancelled because of a passenger's star level or desired destination. Alternately, riders can significantly alter their driver's "status" and potential for future fares with a single bad review. Despite this, the discourse of community, belonging, and opportunity for all remain stalwarts of both the Airbnb and Uber business models. As Roelofsen and Minca (2018) suggest, "the Airbnb platform operationalizes the key concepts of home, community and hospitality by digitally creating a world of real-and-imagined 'hosts' and 'guests' where a specific set of intimate relationships is put on display in the name of a newly conceived global culture of hospitality." Hospitality in Airbnb and Uber thus become more than an ethical imperative. Instead, it operates as a form of social capital, benefiting those who subscribe to narratives of global citizenship, cosmopolitanism, and the chance to be seen as worldly, while expelling those who cannot or will not commit to the particular conditions of community belonging.

THE HOSPITALITY OF GIG ECONOMIES

There is no doubt that hospitality, as an industry, has undergone extraordinary changes in the last decade. From debates over the automation of labour, the impact of the COVID-19 pandemic and, more generally, the future of work in a digital age—the gig or sharing economy is at the forefront of all three. We might think of the gig economy as an inheritor of the network of (often exploitative) foreign worker programmes that have long dominated the service and hospitality industries. Let me be clear, these two systems are intimately connected and what might seem like a new labour regime is not so different from previous answers to the domestic labour shortage in which migrant bodies—and particularly racialized and gendered bodies—have been employed on a temporary and inequitable basis to fill the more undesirable or subservient roles of the hospitality industry, such as construction, housekeeping, cooking, and delivery. Indeed, as Braidotti (2015) notes, "the mechanisms for capture of these bio-labourers, also known as the digital proletariat, follow the classical lines of anthropomorphic difference: the sexualized and racialized 'others', as mentioned above, constitute the core of these new underclasses." In other words, while the methods of procurement may have shifted, the social and labour relations remain the same and rely on latent Orientalist and colonial associations between race, gender, and labour, not to mention conjure power relations that echo that of the Atlantic Slave Trade.

In their work on migrant labour in the gig economy, van Doorn et al. (2020) argue that "without a perpetual influx of migrants, platform companies like Uber, Helpling, Rappi, and Deliveroo would have trouble maintaining their labour supply in many of the cities they operate." As a result, gig and platform labour significantly degrades already sub-par working conditions in which formal and informal work arrangements serve to enhance the bottom line while increasing the vulnerability of those on that *front* line. Such labour platforms thus "engage in selective formalization: a set of business and management practices that formalize some aspects of gig work while perpetuating the precarity associated with informal labour markets" (van Doorn et al. 2020). That these labourers are contractually expected to fulfil roles that continue to put them at risk suggests that hospitality—as both philosophy and practice—is becoming more precarious in an increasingly decentralized and unregulated digital economy. This trend will continue as the future of work shifts away from human labour and towards automation and artificial intelligence, a transition that will undoubtedly see already precarious workers affected disproportionately.

What *has* shifted in the transition from migrant to gig labour is the diminished visibility of such work, an absence that has significant implications for hospitality. In the sharing economy, host and guest rarely meet, other than in the digital universe. Even when sharing the space of a car, rarely is a conversation initiated beyond the confirmation of a name. While we might be tempted to consider this shared space between strangers as an example of pure hospitality, the act of naming, or asking for a name, diminishes that potential. Derrida is clear on this: "absolute hospitality requires that I open up my home and that I give not only give to the foreigner, but to the absolute, unknown, anonymous other, and that I give place to them, that I let them come, that I let them arrive, and take place in the place I offer them, without asking of them either reciprocity (entering into a pact) or even their names" (2000). Similarly, Ikkala and Lampinen's (2015) notion of remote hospitality seems to suggest that hospitality is often less about relations between people than it is about relations between people and space. In other words, it is the site of hospitality that matters, rather than the one who extends it.

Indeed, another significant shift from other forms of hospitality labour is the mobility of relations in gig economies such as those represented by Uber and Airbnb and, if these new relations of hospitality are now often invisible, then they are also simultaneously often mobile. This has significant implications for the future of hospitality, particularly when such a philosophy has often relied on the conventional figures of doors and stoops, thresholds and foyers, as well as the ritual of a host *being at home* to welcome a guest. Even the most philosophically pure conceptions of hospitality—the ones that potentially end in violence or death—are premised on the host being there to greet the arrival, invited or not. And so, when thinking about the hospitality of the gig economy, we must also consider the ways in which the digital "is reshaping the production and experience of space, place, nature, landscape, mobility, and environment" (Ash et al. 2016). The space may be a home, but it may also be a room, a vehicle, a delivery bicycle, an urban tour or other hosted experience, or entirely virtual and contact-free. There is no doubt that digital technologies are changing hospitality, especially those that mediate work and human-economic relations. As Koch and Miles elaborate, scholarship on these new encounters reflects the "profound impacts that digital technologies are having on how people often meet, raising new questions about emerging geographies of home, public and private, the domestic and the urban, and the changing ways that people live and relate to one another in contemporary society" (2020). But hospitality is also changing the digital. The emphasis on community and belonging that both Uber and Airbnb seek to generate is a reminder of human (and perhaps more-than-human) desire to seek connection and to want to feel included and welcomed. And so, while the digital has changed the way we work, play, travel, and even sleep, it is adapting alongside the powerful need for connection and relationality. Hospitality, in other words, is not going anywhere, even as it fails, is mistakenly deployed, is offered conditionally, or is annulled by transactions of reciprocity, finance, reviews, and star status. What it needs is an adaptation that can account for the ways in which relationality is now engaged in a network of assemblages that manifest in off and online spaces, virtual worlds, and techno-mediated encounters, and in ever-shifting digital spaces and identities, while still attending to the strange intimacies that operate at the level of the body and biopolitics.

"Your Ride Has Been Cancelled": Excluding the Other

While hospitality, as an industry, has thrived under the propulsion of the gig economy, absolute hospitality as a philosophical imperative has been curtailed in several notable ways, from the embedded surveillance capitalism within hospitality apps, and their reliance on stars, "superhosts," and reviews; to the platform economy's insistence on anthropomorphic biopolitics and contributions to gentrification and exclusion. As with Siri and Alexa (discussed in Chap. 3), hospitality is unravelled in the context of Uber and Airbnb as they both rely on forms of surveillance (vis-à-vis economic exchange) to which both hosts and guests must tacitly consent to be included in that digital community. Importantly, surveillance capitalism becomes veiled through the language of a platform economy that privileges the discourse of community over the (still non-negotiable) exchange of money. Labour (and its economics) becomes disguised by these narratives of belonging and cosmopolitan citizenship as both platforms try to camouflage the workings of both capitalism and surveillance by individualizing the ethics of care and community and locating them in specific and idealized guest-host relationships. As Roelofsen and Minca (2018) argue, "platforms like Airbnb have in fact turned the labour of care of 'other' bodies in the private sphere into exchange value, engendering more individualized and 'tailor-made' travel experiences, together with the temporary/ephemeral experience of belonging to unknown and distant places." This might seem obvious and commonplace in the context of Uber and Airbnb which, while couching their profit-driven motives in comfy terms, make neither apology nor secret of both operating as platforms for monetary exchange. Both feature immediate cost estimates, for example, for all of the expected charges and fees associated with each service. But the challenge to absolute hospitality vis-à-vis surveillance capitalism is also present in even the more reciprocity-based value systems of other gig economy platforms, such as Couchsurfing which purport to be ostensibly anti-capitalist. As Jenny Germann Molz (2007) explains, when thinking about the notion of reciprocity (rather than commerce) in the Couchsurfing business model, the obligation to repay or compensate in some way, even if not in a monetary sense, seems embedded in a cultural understanding of hospitality and serves "as a contract that extends a binding moral code across the whole community." When participating in Couchsurfing, the exchange of money is not allowed. Other forms of exchange, however, are not only permissible but encouraged. Guests might be urged, for example, to "pay forward" experiences of exemplary hospitality, when they themselves are acting as hosts. Or other forms of reciprocity might be implied, not in the form of material gifts but in shared conversation, social decorum, or cleaning and helping prepare food (Germann Molz 2014). Ultimately, even the non-financial exchanges that find their way into the experience of hospitality suggest that the gig economy relies on a system of implied reciprocity, community behaviour, and trust that are, to be sure, ethical and admirable, but they are not hospitality in its absolute and unconditional form.

Another way that platforms such as Uber and Airbnb disrupt their own narrative of hospitality is through their systems of stars, reviews, and rewards. Reputation is everything in the business of hospitality and both sites rely heavily on both guest and host feedback that quantifies hospitality beyond simply basic services rendered. Reviews can also focus on the "feel" of a place, the welcoming (or perhaps too welcoming) nature of the host or driver, the extent to which a guest understands the social contract of being in another's home or vehicle, and how the ride or stay affected someone's overall travel experience. Roelofsen and Minca suggest that

> review technologies incorporated in a platform are used to police and discipline utopian 'global communities' of travellers, while review-and-ratings mechanisms in tourism have increasingly become parameters of moral behaviour and quality of online- and offline relations. These parameters are based on normative views of 'good hospitality,' or 'core values' of hospitable subjects, and indirectly inform what it means to be a 'good' citizen in a community of travellers. (2018)

The measure of hospitality here, in other words, is often far beyond the host's control and no longer is a clean room or safe ride the standard by which hosts are assessed. Moreover, sometimes the host receives a review or rating without ever being present for the encounter, giving their own reputation over to third-party services, key lock boxes, and pin codes, and potentially missed damage or mess left by previous guests. Reviews also may be alternately positive or negative, depending on how much interaction a guest wants with their host (and how could a host account for the diversity of preferences here?). The reality is that most scenarios unfold as "digitized tourists staying in empty homes and dealing with the standardised instructions left by 'local managers'" who in turn work for larger investors (Roelofsen and Minca 2018). In this review paradigm there is little room for absolute hospitality, and the narratives of welcome, community, and belonging are elided by the powerful metrics that determine who will continue to be successful as a host, based on an invisible set of criteria that changes with every guest.

Airbnb and Uber thus thrive within a discourse of *conditional* hospitality, in which both hosts and guests are bound by a social contract that lays out (whether explicitly, implicitly, or ambiguously) what is required of each. Hosts, for example, are expected to provide high-quality and authentic images of their home or room that are truly representative of the space, to keep the home or vehicle clean and safe, and to be forthcoming about any unexpected factors such as construction noise, roommates, neighbourhood safety, and any non-functioning features (such as appliances) within the home. In turn, guests are expected to abide by the requests of the host around guidelines such as check-in and check-out, cleaning, respecting noise restrictions, or replacing standard pantry items if they run out. These are often viewed as norms rather than strict rules, the consequences being poor reviews rather than punitive or financial punishment. Airbnb operates under what they call "host reliability standards," which include four pillars of proper hosting: host commitment (honouring bookings), listing cleanliness, listing accuracy, and host communication (Airbnb 2022). Failure to meet these standards can result in a range of actions taken against hosts, but Airbnb first encourages hosts and guests to try and solve any problems themselves, before any official violations are reported. For Germann Molz (2007), these community or host standards might not be legally binding, but they nonetheless discipline hosts and guests on an almost panoptic level. In her words, "the reputation systems on these websites act as a kind of surveillance mechanism that monitors this reciprocity between hosts and guests, but that also secures the face-to-face meeting between strangers and controls the boundaries of the hospitality community." Ultimately, star systems, and the veiled threat or surveillance vis-á-vis community guidelines not only turn the hospitality of the platform economy into a conditional one. What's more, they actively prevent hospitality from taking place at all, cancelling the possibility of an ethical encounter before it even has a chance to occur. What makes Airbnb and Uber, then, with their model of pre-emptive annulment, such an abdication of hospitality is the evacuation of the true stranger from any level of encounter. Hospitality is thus datafied and ultimately forestalled by the conditional algorithms already in place—those that sort, rank, and identify—before the meeting can ever occur.

Beyond the systems of rewards and reputation that determine what constitutes a good host or guest, there are other forms of privilege and exclusion that highlight the intersection of race and class in the larger discourses of the gig economy and prove another challenge to hospitable welcome. Within the context of Uber, for example, racial discrimination has the potential of occurring from both sides. While Uber claims to offer both drivers (hosts) and riders (guests) with anti-racism resources (including unconscious bias training for customer support staff) and a zero-tolerance anti-racism policy within their community guidelines (Uber 2022), there is no doubt that racial inequality is not only an ongoing problem in the interaction between drivers and riders; it might actually be embedded in the algorithm itself. In 2021, reports emerged in the UK that the facial recognition software drivers are required to upload their photo could not "read" darker skin tones (see Barry 2021; Butler 2021; Azeez 2021). In many of these cases, when the Microsoft-powered API[7] software did not recognize a dark skin tone, drivers were given a message that they had "improperly used" the Uber application and were blocked from the platform (Barry 2021). But if we are tempted to believe this was a one-off tech problem or computer glitch, we also have to consider the reports that some drivers have received a lower rating from a passenger due to their local language proficiency, race, or accent, regardless of how the actual ride went. While filing a lawsuit on behalf of drivers dismissed for low ratings in the US, attorney Shannon Liss-Riordan charged: "Uber's use of this system to determine driver terminations constitutes race discrimination, as it is widely recognized that customer evaluations of workers are frequently racially biased" (Allyn 2020). That drivers within the Uber network are racialized, yet still must accept fares from passengers who might give them low ratings might be an example of pure hospitality, in that the welcome is extended even to risky or "bad" guests. But what is good for philosophy is not always good for politics, and certainly not good

[7] Application Programming Interface.

for racial justice. If anything, the potential for racism within the platform reminds us of the precarity of both host and guests and the level of risk both parties must assume when entering into a hospitality pact on which their livelihood often depends.

Racism is also a problem for Airbnb, where hosts can pre-emptively deny a booking based on set of parameters of their choosing. While often disguised with justification around unavailable dates, the unsuitability of accommodation for a certain number of guests, or perhaps raising rates before confirming a reservation, there is nothing to stop hosts from excluding certain guests on the basis of race. Edelman et al. (2017) confirm: "in the early stage of negotiation between hosts and guests, questions like age, health, nationality, sexual orientation, skin colour may be key in selecting the people who may sleep in their homes." Whether hosts base this decision on a profile photo of a potential guest, their city or country of origin, or a "foreign-sounding" name,[8] there is a racial hierarchy at work in the hospitality practices of Airbnb. Returning to the recent "Strangers" ad which began this chapter, there are clearly attempts being made by Airbnb to promote itself as not only anti-racist, but accepting of strangers everywhere, carefully crafting statement around how and why a host might not accept a booking. On their website they suggest: "A booking is more likely to be confirmed when the host and guest preferences are a good fit. That's why our search algorithms are designed to match guests to spaces that are right for their trip, and hosts to booking opportunities that are right for their hosting preferences" (Airbnb 2022). In such a statement, what appears as a welcome of strangers is actually a carefully constructed list of identifiers that make that stranger *less* strange. Here, Airbnb embraces the concept of hospitality but sidesteps the law. Absolute hospitality, contrary to this discourse of "a good fit," is not given on the basis of sameness or commonality—whether a shared culture, language, or set of holiday preferences—but on the basis of difference. Absolute hospitality not only welcomes the other but allows that other to remain strange.

---

[8] In their 2017 study, Edelman, Luca, and Svirsky found "widespread discrimination" against guests with distinctively African American names. According to their fieldwork that used false names to inquire into the availability of 6400 separate Airbnb listings across five American cities, they found that "African American guests received a positive response roughly 42 percent of the time, compared to roughly 50 percent for white guests" (2017). What's more is that they discovered that hosts who reject a booking from African American guests ended up willingly losing an average of 65–100 USD in missed revenue rather than welcoming a racialized guest into their home.

For Rosi Braidotti (2013), this process of achieving compatibility signifies a "systematized standard of recognisability," aimed at achieving a degree of "Sameness" or, what Airbnb would highlight as, the "best match." Thus, while recognizability is a cancellation of pure hospitality, it is a condition of Airbnb. Such practices reflect what Germann Molz (2014) calls "homophily—a tendency to connect with people who are like us—[which] is a common feature in online social networks." Ultimately then, the laws of Airbnb subscribe to a conditional version of hospitality that uses its language but forgoes its most absolute imperative.

Marginalization and exclusion are thus a problem within many aspects of the gig or platform economy and often operate in an ecosystem already primed for profit. I am speaking here of the ways in which capitalism literally moves people into marginalized positions. As Braidotti argues, "given that the political economy of global capitalism consists in multiplying and distributing differences for the sake of profit, it produces ever-shifting waves of genderization and sexualization, racialization and naturalization of multiple 'others'" (2015). Perhaps this is best exemplified in the concept of gentrification, of which Airbnb has faced countless accusations. What is curious about gentrification here, beyond its obvious relevance to processes of racial discrimination and exclusion within the booking process, is its particular targeting of low-income and racialized neighbourhoods that have been historically vibrant but woefully underserved within advanced neoliberal capitalism. According to Barker (2020), "the so-called 'Airbnb effect' on local housing markets has grown into a significant cause for concern, particularly when looking at its impacts on housing stock, prices and communities" (Barker 2020). Indeed, several studies have shown that the rise of properties converted into short-term rental units, primarily through the Airbnb platform, has resulted in decrease in housing supply for local residents, an increase in long-term rental rates, and an overall "pricing out" effect on existing renters *and* homeowners who can now no longer afford to live in the neighbourhoods they settled in due to the cost of living increases brought in via the tourist and short-term letting sector (see Barker 2020, Waschsmuth and Weisler 2018; Mermet 2017; Bivens 2019; Bernardi 2018). The irony here should be immediately clear: existing hosts/residents are pushed out of their spaces of hosting in order to make room for the platform economy's version of hospitality. And what might tentatively offer a productive new thinking about a hospitality—that which is untethered from hearth and home, and discontinuous in the sense of and ever-shifting landscape of communities, hosts, and guests—is producing the very effects absolute hospitality seeks to ameliorate: home*less*ness, exclusion, and hostility. Let us also remember that these discourses of exclusion and redevelopment happen alongside the platform's explicit campaigning for social justice, diversity, and inclusion. This irony is enhanced when we realize that the very figures Airbnb seeks to immortalize through song in their advertisement are subject to these exact forms of gentrification and displacement. Indeed, the tragedy of Freddie Gray, which began this chapter and to whom Airbnb pays homage, was recently compounded in Baltimore, where the housing project in which he grew up was targeted for demolition (Toronto City News 2020). Despite the site's attention as a protest and gathering ground for Black Lives Matter supporters, the City of Baltimore's assurance to "relocate" residents is a thin attempt at glossing over the language of gentrification. Indeed, as Nathan Connolly (2018), who studies housing history, confirms, "urban renewal has always promised improvement in the lives of poor black folks. But the fact is, once you move these people out, they're out of sight" (Connolly in Anft 2018). Whether through gentrification of police violence, people of colour are being erased and it seems a cruel paradox to invoke racial justice on one hand while benefitting from the effects of (often racialized) redevelopment on the other. Suddenly Airbnb's claim that "we are all strangers" seems, at best, blissfully naïve and, at worst, a poor attempt at misdirection away from the company's role in gentrification and violence.

Hospitality and Platform Biopolitics

Operating alongside the challenges posed by the rituals of capitalism, the conditional acceptance of guests and hosts, and the realities of racial exclusion and gentrification, hospitality is ultimately elided through the platform economy's dependence on biopolitics and anthropomorphism. While the biopolitical is a fraught term, historically understood in tandem with Foucauldian discipline or "technologies of power" (1976), in the context of hospitality and digital life, Hardt and Negri provide both a useful and tidy definition. In their reasoning, biopolitics concerns "the production of social life itself, in which the economic, the political and the cultural increasingly overlap and invest one another" (Hardt and Negri 2010). Here, the biological and social are intimately and irrevocably linked. Indeed, rather than facilitating a hospitable and welcoming encounter between strangers who are unknown, both Uber and Airbnb thrive on knowing as much as possible, turning relational bodies into data-fied ones, as information gleaned by these platforms is generated through a range of devices that record people's movements through space, locations, behaviour, communication, appearance, and many other aspects of their daily lives (see Lupton 2017). The knowledge (data) generated from these hospitality platforms carries an even greater currency than that which is exchanged for the services themselves. And if, as Braidotti (2013) suggests, "contemporary capitalism is 'bio-political' in that it aims at controlling all that lives," this is deeply the case in regard to the information generated by Uber and Airbnb that is used to create recommendations, targeted promotions, and encouragements to increase status within the platform. For Uber and Airbnb, therefore, hospitality depends on data, not relationality. Data is, in fact, the "the lifeblood of the business" (Rosenbush 2014), a curious use of language that suggests the biopolitical is at the "heart" of platform hospitality at the same time as it affirms the bio-anthropomorphism and human-centred nature of encounter. Indeed, as Roelofsen and Minca (2018) argue, the reputational and review metrics of the platform are "translated in the language of biopolitics," reducing the act of hospitality to an individualizing narrative in which each guest and host are answerable for themselves only, rather than responsible to the other.

The biopolitical "horizon" (Roelofsen and Minca 2018) of the gig economy narrative is, of course, the "superhost": someone "who goes above and beyond in their hosting duties and is a shining example of how a Host should be" (Airbnb 2022). The superhost is, in fact, exaggerated in its visibility on the Airbnb booking site: bumped to the top of the list with a "Superhost" tag over the image of the space, and displaying a colourful badge next to their profile. Rather than promote interactions between unknown and unidentifiable others, superhosts are hyper-visible in virtual space yet still almost entirely absent from the physical experience of hosting once their guest arrives. In fact, the sub-line under the search filter for selecting only Superhost spaces reads "Stay with *recognized* hosts" (my emphasis), reinforcing the message that, for Airbnb, hospitality is best when familiar and vetted; in other words, when it is less strange. Rather than adhere to the fundamental principles of absolute hospitality in which naming and recognition are antithetical then, Airbnb goes "far beyond this veil of anonymity by "individualizing (and ranking) the heroic figure of the host" (Roelofsen and Minca 2018). It is easy to see how the Superhost designation might assuage fears of guests who are slowly wading back into the waters of travel following two years of pandemic lockdowns at the same time as it highlights the biopolitical as sustained by individual responsibility. Clearly, the disruption and upheaval in travel caused by COVID-19 has amplified the individualization and ranking of both guests and hosts by crossing the biopolitical line one step further, turning the disciplinary and scrutinizing (conditional) lens from the outward performance of the host body (cleanliness, location, amenities) to its internal processing and health (not-contagious). Not only have both guests and hosts been subject to a range of additional conditions to ensure a stay or passage could be completed, for instance providing hand sanitizer, extra cleaning and disinfecting practices, and enforcing mask wearing, etc; they have also had to disclose test results and/or vaccination status, subjecting not just the outer characteristics of a guest but also their most intimate, internal, viral, and immunitary selves. Indeed, in an ironic turn, while facilitating the return to travel and revival of the hospitality industry, the vaccine passport or status document has perhaps been the greatest biopolitical foreclosure of absolute hospitality since the border security regimes initiated after 9/11. Thus, what appears to be virtual is actually intensely corporeal and biological as both guest and host bodies are disciplined into a kind of hospitable docility—one that consents to not only identification but also medical recording, health data surveillance, and contact tracing to ensure that not only the individual subject is "safe" to be a guest or host, but their chain of relationality is also secure. To be clear, these procedures are highlighted and accelerated in the context of global pandemic but they are not new. Rather than creating hospitable relations, Airbnb and Uber function, in the very building blocks of their platform DNA, to create disciplined bodies, and they mobilize not only the provision of a ride or a room, but also what it means to be a good citizen.

RISKY HOSPITALITY: SPACE AND STRANGER INTIMACIES

Despite some of the challenges outlined above, which would seem to cancel the welcome of strangers before it even has opportunity to begin, the premise of both the Uber and Airbnb platforms remains remarkably attuned to the project of hospitality and reminds us of both the instability and the potential intimacy, of relations between strangers. Here, hospitality is not so much a matter of human-computer interaction but of digitally facilitated *human-human* interaction. Moreover, these apps (and gaps) also prompt us to think about the forms of intimacy generated by technology *beyond* kinship and the hetero-relationality of dating applications. Hospitality is a strange intimacy whereby—in the context of gig economy apps—the digital is inextricable from the relations we have, and the world we inhabit. The spatiality of digital encounters between strangers is simultaneously distant (mediated by a screen) but at the same time more embodied than ever, and part of a complex web of relations with ourselves, with others, and with our environment. In the context of hospitality, Uber and Airbnb are anything but straightforward; instead, they inform and animate the loci of intimacy as tenuous and complex, spatial, and situated (whether virtual or material) and challenge the stability of a philosophy of hospitality that demands not only a host who is at home, but the concept of a home at all. Instead, Uber and Airbnb ask us to think about "stranger intimacy" being "defined broadly as conditional relations of openness among the unacquainted, however fleeting, through which affective structures of knowing, providing, befriending or even loving are built" (Koch and Miles 2020). Yet what seems to be more interesting in these platforms of stranger intimacies is the lengths that both hosts and guests go to *avoid* intimacy altogether. A name given to an Uber driver might suggest a kind of engaged introduction, but in reality, it is the last words the pair will likely speak to one another. Similarly, the Airbnb host often works diligently to avoid interactions with the guest, offering remote entry and exit instructions even in cases where they happen to be home. For a form of hospitality that is so dependent on a particular space, these strangers never actually share that space together. Alternatively, host and guest may feel disappointed by the lack of interaction in their experience. As Bialski (2012) recognizes, "negotiating interaction between strangers, hosting and being hosted, entering a stranger's private home, avoiding intimacy, anticipating closeness, becoming attached and then detached—these are all skills people have to acquire and adapt to as they increasingly become mobile and come into contact with mobile others." As Bialski infers, hospitality is becoming not only increasingly mobile, but also increasingly unstable, untethered from the formal relations whereby a host welcomes a guest, allows them passage through the door, and offers them food, drink, and shelter. Instead, the gig economy shows us the precarity of these host and guest identities, not to mention the precarity of sovereign space and the extent to which the initial welcome can forge (or force) both willed and unwilled forms of intimacy.

Also unwilled may be the more dangerous forms of intimacy that the gig or platform economy potentializes. Indeed, intimate hospitalities between strangers may move us towards an ethic of welcoming the stranger, but may also reify the necessity of boundaries between self and other, inside and out, lest some relations result in violence. It seems to be the case that stranger intimacies are perhaps simultaneously the most risky *and* most ethical of all. And while Uber and Airbnb can be held up as examples of the potential of hospitable relations between strangers, they should not be overly sentimentalized—as Airbnb's "Strangers" ad would have us believe. Indeed, Valentine calls for studies of these intimate spaces to avoid any romanticization of the possibilities of encounter and instead consider more critically how different forms of contact may translate into attitudes of respect for difference, but equally may leave intolerant values unmoved or even hardened (in Koch and Miles 2020). If anything, these "strange" intimacies do more for establishing the self than they do for welcoming the stranger, particularly when recognition is used as a condition for entry or service. As Koefoed and Simonsen (2011) argue, "every time we meet the 'undecidables' we seek to re-establish ways of recognition, not only by reading the body of this particular 'stranger' but also by trying to tell the difference between him/her and other strangers." I want to emphasize the "re" establish here—as these gestures of recognition are nothing new and instead already structured by existing social codes of conduct around what to do when meeting someone new. Any intimacy potentialized by this space is thus already preformed before the encounter, based on a scripted political and cultural conditioning (we might say coding) of how we are taught to respond to strangers.

Regardless, hospitality, especially in the platform economy, is an ephemeral relation—and the stranger is a temporary condition. In every encounter with Uber and Airbnb, there is a wager to be made and a transformation from a stranger into either an 'other' or an 'intimate.' But let us not presume that by becoming an 'intimate' the stranger is not dislodged from a possible violence. Indeed, as Germann Molz (2014) recognizes, "although intimacy connotes a kind of rose-coloured warmth, closeness is not always cosy. Intimacy can also involve vulnerability and suffocation. While network hospitality can produce deeply meaningful, trustful, and transformative encounters, not all meetings unfold in quite such idyllic terms." And herein lies the paradox of hospitality *par excellence*. The potential for violence—and certainly the act of violence—in the encounter between guest and host in the gig economy severs the social contract but advances hospitality in its absolute and philosophical pursuit. In other words, hospitality remains philosophically pure but politically problematic. We can easily glance further back into the histories of physical hosting (such as those in the Abrahamic or Homeric traditions) to see how hospitality is both announced and annulled in regard to gender and the antiquated (and contemporary) traditions of not only expecting women to fulfil the material conditions of the hospitality pact but also offering them up as gifts for hosts as discussed in Chap. 3.

In her provocative chapter "Baiting Hospitality," Irina Aristarkhova recounts a story in which an experiment in gender, travel, and hospitality confirms that the risk of encounter is especially fraught for women. In 2008, performance artists Pippa Bacca and Silvia Moro set off on a European hitchhiking adventure, wearing only wedding dresses in an attempt to demonstrate peace and trust within the travelling community, and the world (see Tanga 2017; Aristarkhova 2015). Documenting their journey in various media forms, they named the project "Brides on Tour" and, while intending to meet in Beirut and then Jerusalem for a final exhibition, became separated in Turkey. Two weeks after going missing, Bacca's raped and strangled body was found, and the man responsible, Murat Karataş, was located shortly thereafter when he attempted to use her phone card (Aristarkhova 2015). Interestingly, when speaking about her death, Bacca's family invoked the language of hospitality to suggest that the artist was not simply naïve but, rather, had "such radical openness to the Other" (in Aristarkhova 2015). It seems hard to find philosophical purity, even ethical potential, in such violent circumstances, particularly when, once again, it is the body of a woman doing hospitality work here. In its tragic outcome, Bacca and Moro's experiment makes clear the need to consider both Airbnb and Uber as a form of platform economy punctuated by risk. Combining the trust in stranger narrative of Airbnb with the ride-hailing physical space of Uber and its contemporaries, the philosophy behind "Brides of Tour" meets at the intersection of intimacy, space, and risk where hospitality paradoxically succeeds and then fails. It is also, it should be noted, not as sensational a story as we might think. Bacca's death is important and demonstrates the deep inconsistencies of hospitality, but hers is not an exceptional case. Not only is violence against women while ride-sharing or hitchhiking well-documented in new stories around the world; it is also not a stretch to assume that many reading this have, like myself, taken the risks Bacca did or, at the very least, used our Uber apps to follow the map closely on our phones when accepting a ride alone.

Despite these potential dangers, it is hard to not be struck, and even ethically mobilized, by Derrida's formulation of absolute hospitality that relies on an unconditional opening up to the unknown stranger. This unconditional hospitality is offered without knowing the stranger's name or identity, without expectations of repayment, and regardless of the risks the stranger might pose (see Derrida 1999, 2000). This is precisely the ethical opening Bacca sought to achieve and to prove possible. While Moro showed more hesitancy when getting into vehicles that raised alarm, Bacca "by contrast, followed the law of unconditional hospitality: one says "yes" to anyone and anything that comes" (Aristarkhova 2015). Regardless of how their stories ended—one in death and the other forever ceasing to create art (see Cesareo 2018), this story of "Brides on Tour" suggests that, whether as hosts or guests, the spaces of hospitality are irrevocably more risky for women, and the concept of stranger intimacy must be exposed as a too-easy slip into violence where women bear the brunt of hospitality's failed promises.

Conclusion: Affirmations of Hospitality and Biopolitics

In 2020, Uber launched its controversial anti-racism campaign across multiple platforms including social media and billboards across 13 US cities. The timing of this was meant to coincide with the anniversary of Martin Luther King Jr's "I Have a Dream" speech and the campaign featured the slogan: "If you tolerate racism, delete Uber" (Zelaya 2020). While it is hard to critique any initiative that uses a wide-reaching global platform to propel a social justice message, Uber's timing is curious here, clearly reacting to the ongoing Black Lives Matter movement but at a time when the company was fighting behind the scenes to deny its drivers (many of whom are people of colour) benefits or a living wage (Mahdawi 2020). Much like the Airbnb "Strangers" ad discussed at the beginning of this chapter, the attempt by Uber to drive customers to its service through socially conscious advertising is an aggressive tactic that elides the darker and inhospitable underbelly of the gig economy. It is, however, part of a much larger campaign, shared across hospitality platforms, that celebrates the almost ubiquitous twenty-first-century concept of global citizenship. In Uber's 2022 Diversity, Equity, and Inclusion report, CEO Dara Khosrowshahi writes: "we can't just hope that our products alone will improve equity and fairness. We must use our global breadth, our technology and our data to help make change, faster—so that we become a more actively anti-racist company; a safer, more inclusive company and platform; and a faithful ally to all the communities we serve." Here, instead of acknowledging the role that advanced global capitalism, data surveillance, the replacement of human labour, and new technology has played in inequity worldwide, Khosrowshahi instead proposes these as the *antidote* to injustice. Moreover, the gesture towards a global citizenship, or cosmopolitanism, offers a version of hospitality that operates *with* surveillance capitalism rather than against it, suggesting that such forms of citizenship and belonging are little more than the coming together of millions of disciplined and biopolitical bodies and identities.

Despite this, both Uber and Airbnb still manage to tell us something new about hospitality, and there is potentially something instructive here for our digital lives, even if it is found in the failure to maintain an unconditional ethic of welcome. From the gig economy, for example, we are reminded that now, more than ever, hospitality is networked. It is mobile, taken out of the private home and spread across cities, landscapes, vehicles, and spare rooms, and across virtual and physical spaces. It is moving, in the language of Uber, "at the incredible speed of now" (Uber 2022). Moreover, hospitality is disrupted. It is undone by the contracts of reciprocity and payment and then put together anew by reversing hospitality's primary relationship—that of guest and host—and resists their definition as distant and stable identities. Instead, guests now take over a kitchen and prepare a meal for their hosts, and hosts leave a key for their guests and abandon their home completely. Moreover, on many platforms (i.e. Couchsurfing), one must be a host in order to be a guest. The two are not only interchangeable but paradoxically, even parasitically, entwined—hosting cannot exist without the guest and vice versa and, indeed, one person can be both at the same time. Indeed, in digital hospitality, we move back and forth between what David Bell (2007) calls "flickering moments of hosting and guesting."

Rather than arguing for the impossibility of hospitality altogether, or even for the elimination of biopolitics, I want to suggest a kind of *thinking-with* these strange and new networks between humans, data, space, and other forms of life borne out of relations in the platform economy. Such a move prompts us to consider the potentially emancipatory shift to what Agamben and others have termed "affirmative biopolitics," where the biopolitical is recognized as an alternative domain of empowerment rather than oppression (see Berlant 2004, 2011; Braidotti 2013, 2015; Agamben 2000; Esposito 2008). In Hardt and Negri's words, we might think of the diffusion of power through examples such as Airbnb as the "decentered and deterritorializing apparatus of rule that progressively incorporates the entire global realm within its open, expanding frontiers" (2010). For Hardt and Negri, while this dispersion of power is, to be sure, a hallmark of globalization, it also offers up new opportunities for subversion and resistance. Similarly, as Braidotti (2013) confirms, "affirmative politics combines critique with creativity in the pursuit of alternative visions and projects." Hardt and Negri (2010) also offer a poignant conceptualization of affirmative biopolitics that has deep resonance with the project of hospitality. For them, such affirmation "takes on the contours of an ecology of the common." Such language seems to oddly echo the discourse of belonging in both Uber and Airbnb's version of a hospitable global community, as both seem to promote re-drawing the global map as a utopian vision of sharing and stranger-friendship. Even though these platforms rely simultaneously on problematic metrics of individual achievement and global community, might they still offer a new way of thinking about the "contours" of the common? Or about the ways that decentralization and sharing (however fraughtly conceived) might initiate, in Catherine Mills' words, "a non-homogenous, non-exclusive creative force upon which Empire rests, but which also has the power to constitute alternative political and social forms of life"? (2017).

Can hospitality, then, provide an example of affirmative biopolitics? It is, undoubtedly, an ethic in desperate need of radical rethinking. Braidotti's ideas around posthuman biopolitics are also useful here, as the ways in which guests and hosts are constructed in platform hospitality rely more on a reduction of the individual into data rather than the humanist forms of disciplinary power upon which most genealogies of the biopolitical are based. In Braidotti's (2015) words: "The central discrepancy between Foucault's notion of biopower and contemporary posthuman political structures has to do with the displacement of anthropocentrism. I argued that the biogenetic structure of advanced capitalism reduces bodies to carriers of vital information, which get invested with financial value and capitalized." Thinking about the investiture of the body as data rather than as species is central to this entire volume's insistence on a post- or more-than-human hospitality and how affirmative biopolitics might offer an alternative to the inhospitable nature of advanced capitalism within the gig economy. For Braidotti, "ethical relations create possible worlds by mobilizing resources that have been left untapped in the present, including our desires and imagination" (Braidotti 2015). Perhaps philosophical hospitality is the resource we have been looking for that, combined with posthuman and affirmative biopolitics, might shift not only the narrative around what it means to truly welcome strangers but also around how a politics of care can work to resist the hostility of anthropomorphic ethics and late-stage capitalism.

In his "Third Definitive Article" in *Towards Perpetual Peace*, Immanuel Kant offers a model for hospitality that echoes much of the idealist narrative of the gig economy—that is, the promotion of "global citizenship." In Kant's words, all "men" have a right to temporary visitation "by virtue of their common possession of the surface of the earth, where, as a globe, they cannot infinitely disperse and hence must finally tolerate the presence of each other" (Kant 1795). Yet curiously, he begins his essay with a musing about a sign on a Dutch inn. The sign, perhaps glanced upon by a weary traveller, depicts a graveyard at the same time as it advertises "perpetual peace." Kant is quick to point out the satire here—is this sign meant for those who love war, or the philosophers who "cherish the sweet dream" of peace (Kant 1795)? Perhaps the peace in question here is not the absence of war but, rather the endless sleep of death, the innkeeper's sign gesturing to the only condition upon which true and perpetual peace might be found. Here, thinking about what is perhaps philosophy's first Airbnb, Kant establishes both the conditions and consequences of hospitality. Hospitality may indeed be a "question of right" rather than charity (Kant 1795), but it is also conditioned by the "peaceable behaviour" of the guest, reminding us that while hospitality-towards-death may be pure, the only hospitality that can truly be offered is one that takes into account the reality (and materiality) of living in a world with strangers—and not just human ones. In this way, Kant's hospitality is far from pure but proceeds in David L. Clark's words "as if peace were possible" (in Redfield 2009).

In other words, what would hospitality look like that remained radically open to difference while attending to the ways in which both hosting and guesting are differentially experienced in an increasingly digitalized but always already inequitable world? As such, perhaps Uber and Airbnb are not occasions to abolish the promise of an absolute hospitality, but rather to allow it to take on new shapes and (life)forms, and to let it grow in ways that attend to the very real and material consequences of a set of ethics that is irrevocably more risky for some. We are on the cusp of a future that demands we rethink how hospitality operates in a gig economy, and in digital life at large, that is, only becoming more complex, extensive, rhizomatic, ubiquitous, and mobile. It demands we consider hospitality in new ways, in *more-than-human* ways and, indeed, as if it might, still, be possible.

REFERENCES

Agamben, Giorgio. 2000. *Means without End: Notes on Politics*. Minneapolis: University of Minnesota Press.

Airbnb. 2020. We Stand with #BlackLivesMatter. *Twitter*. https://twitter.com/airbnb/status/1267536619164151808?lang=en-GB.

———. 2021. Strangers Extended Cut. *YouTube*. https://www.youtube.com/watch?v=swC5HX1HmLw.

Airbnb.com. 2022. *Airbnb Inc*.

Allyn, Bobby. 2020. Uber Fires Drivers Based on 'Racially Biased' Star Rating System, Lawsuit Claims. *NPR*. https://www.npr.org/2020/10/26/9278 51281/uber-fires-drivers-based-on-racially-biased-star-rating-system-lawsuit-claims.

Anft, Michael. 2018. Three Years After His Death, Freddie Gray's Neighborhood Faces a New Loss. *Bloomberg*. https://www.bloomberg.com/news/articles/2018-04-19/an-unsentimental-end-for-freddie-gray-s-housing-complex.

Aristarkhova, Irina. 2015. Baiting Hospitality. In *Security and Hospitality in Literature and Culture: Modern and Contemporary Perspectives*, ed. Jeffrey Clapp and Emily Ridge. New York: Routledge.

Ash, James, Rob Kitchin, and Agnieszka Leszczynski. 2016. Digital Turn, Digital Geographies? *Progress in Human Geography* 42 (1). https://doi.org/10.1177/0309132516664800.

Azeez, Walé. 2021. Uber Faces Legal Action in UK Over Racial Discrimination Claims. *CNN Business*. https://edition.cnn.com/2021/10/07/tech/uber-racism-uk-lawsuit-facial-recognition/index.html.

Barker, Gary. 2020. The Airbnb Effect on Housing and Rent. *Forbes*. https://www.forbes.com/sites/garybarker/2020/02/21/the-Airbnb-effect-on-housing-and-rent/.

Barron, Justine. 2020. Freddie Gray, Five Years Later. *The Appeal*. https://theappeal.org/freddie-gray-five-years-later/.

Barry, Eloise. 2021. Uber Drivers Say a 'Racist' Algorithm is Putting Them Out of Work. *Time*. https://time.com/6104844/uber-facial-recognition-racist/.

Bell, David. 2007. Moments of Hospitality. In *Mobilizing Hospitality: The Ethics of Social Relations in a Mobile World*, ed. Jennie Germann Molz and Sarah Gibson, 29–44. Aldershot: Ashgate.

Berlant, Lauren. 2004. Critical Inquiry, Affirmative Culture. *Critical Inquiry* 30 (2). https://doi.org/10.1086/421150.

———. 2011. *Cruel Optimism*. Durham: Duke University Press.

Bernardi, Monica. 2018. The Impact of Airbnb on our Cities: Gentrification and 'Disneyfication' 2.0. *The Urban Media Lab*. https://labgov.city/theurbanmedialab/the-impact-of-Airbnb-on-our-cities-gentrification-and-disneyfication-2-0/.

Bhuiyan, Johana. 2017. Everything you Need to Know About Uber's Turbulent 2017. *Vox*. https://www.vox.com/2017/8/20/16164176/uber-2017-timeline-scandal.

Bialski, Paula. 2012. *Becoming Intimately Mobile*. New York: Peter Lang.

Bivens, Josh. 2019. The Economic Costs and benefits of Airbnb. *Economic Policy Institute*. Washington, D.C. https://files.epi.org/pdf/157766.pdf.

Braidotti, Rosi. 2013. *The Posthuman*. Cambridge: Polity.

———. 2015. Posthuman Affirmative Biopolitics. In *Resisting Biopolitics: Philosophical, Political, and Performative Strategies*, ed. S.E. Wilmer and Audronė Žukauskaitė. New York: Routledge.

Butler, Sarah. 2021. Uber Facing New UK Driver Claims of Racial Discrimination. *The Guardian*. https://www.theguardian.com/technology/2021/oct/06/uber-facing-new-uk-driver-claims-of-racial-discrimination.

Cesareo, Matilde. 2018. Artist—Silvia Moro. *Yes, No, and More*. Exhibition. https://yesandmoreno.wordpress.com/2018/09/25/artist-silvia-moro/.

Chesky, Brian. 2022. *Twitter*. https://twitter.com/bchesky.

Couchsurfing.com. 2022. *Couchsurfing International Inc*.

Derrida, Jacques. 1999. *Adieu to Emmanuel Levinas*. Translated by Pascale-Anne Brault and Michael Naas. Stanford University Press.

———. 2000. Hostipitality. *Angelaki: Journal of the Theoretical Humanities* 5 (3). https://doi.org/10.1080/09697250020034706.

van Doorn, Niels, Fabian Ferrari, and Mark Graham. 2020. Migration and Migrant Labour in the Gig Economy: An Intervention. Available at SSRN: https://ssrn.com/abstract=3622589 or https://doi.org/10.2139/ssrn.3622589.

Edelman, Benjamin, Michael Luca, and Dan Svirsky. 2017. Racial Discrimination in the Sharing Economy: Evidence from a Field Experiment. *American Economic Association* 9 (2). https://doi.org/10.1257/app.20160213.

Esposito, Robert. 2008. *Bios: Biopolitics and Philosophy*. Minneapolis, MN: University of Minnesota Press.

Germann Molz, Jennie. 2007. Cosmopolitans on the Couch: Mobile Hospitality and the Internet. In *Mobilizing Hospitality: The Ethics of Social Relations in a Mobile World*, ed. Jennie Germann Molz and Sarah Gibson. Routledge.

———. 2014. Toward a Network Hospitality. *First Monday* 19 (3). https://firstmonday.org/ojs/index.php/fm/article/view/4824/3848.

Hardt, Michael, and Antonio Negri. 2010. *Commonwealth*. Cambridge: Harvard.

Ikkala, Tapio, and Airi Lampinen. 2015. Monetizing Network Hospitality: Hospitality and Sociability in the Context of Airbnb. In *Proceedings of the 18th ACM Conference on Computer Supported Cooperative Work & Social Computing.* ACM, New York, NY. https://doi.org/10.1145/2675133.2675274.

Iqbal, Mansoor. 2022. Uber Revenue and Usage Statistics. *Business of Apps.* https://www.businessofapps.com/data/uber-statistics/.

Kant, Immanuel. 1915 (1795). *Perpetual Peace, a Philosophical Essay.* Translated by M. Campbell Smith. London, G. Allen & Unwin ltd.

Kassam, Ashifa. 2017. Uber Threatens to Leave Quebec in Protest at New Rules for Drivers. *The Guardian.* https://www.theguardian.com/technology/2017/sep/26/uber-threatens-leave-quebec-drivers.

Koch, Regan, and Sam Miles. 2020. Inviting the Stranger In: Intimacy, Digital Technology and New Geographies of Encounter. *Progress in Human Geography* 45 (6). https://journals.sagepub.com/doi/10.1177/0309132520961881.

Koefoed, Lasse, and Kirsten Simonsen. 2011. 'The Stranger', the City and the Nation: On the Possibilities of Identification and Belonging. *European and Regional Studies* 18 (4): 1–15.

LaFrance, Adrienne. 2017. Uber Did What!?: A Field Guide to the Company's Ongoing PR Nightmare. *The Atlantic.* https://www.theatlantic.com/technology/archive/2017/04/ubers-pr-nightmare-a-field-guide/523269/.

Lashley, Conrad, and Alison J. Morrison, eds. 2000. *In Search of Hospitality: Theoretical Perspectives and Debates.* Boston: Butterworth Heinemann.

Levin, Sam. 2017. Uber's Scandals, Blunders and PR Disasters: The Full List. *The Guardian.* https://www.theguardian.com/technology/2017/jun/18/uber-travis-kalanick-scandal-pr-disaster-timeline.

Lupton, Deborah. 2017. Feeling Your Data: Touch and Making Sense of Personal Digital Data. *New Media & Society* 19 (10). https://doi.org/10.1177/1461444817717515.

Mahdawi, Arwa. 2020. Sorry, Uber. Anti-racism Slogans are all Very Well—but How About Paying a Decent Wage. *The Guardian.* https://www.theguardian.com/commentisfree/2020/sep/09/sorry-uber-anti-racism-slogans-are-all-very-well-but-how-about-paying-a-decent-wage.

Mermet, Anne-Cécile. 2017. Airbnb and Tourism Gentrification: Critical Insights from the Exploratory Analysis of the 'Airbnb syndrome' in Reykjavík. In *Tourism and Gentrification in Contemporary Metropolises,* ed. Maria Gravari-Barbas and Sandra Guinard. London: Routledge.

Mills, Catherine. 2017. *Biopolitics.* Routledge.

Morby, Kevin. 2020. Beautiful Strangers/No Place to Fall. *Oh Mon Dieu: Live à Paris.* Dead Oceans.

N.a. 2020. Housing Project Where Freddie Gray Lived Being Torn Down. *Toronto City News.* https://toronto.citynews.ca/2020/04/17/housing-project-where-freddie-gray-lived-being-torn-down/.

Redfield, Marc. 2009. *The Rhetoric of Terror: Reflections on 9/11 and the War on Terror*. New York: Fordham University Press.

Roelofsen, Maartje, and Claudio Minca. 2018. The Superhost. Biopolitics, Home and Community in the Airbnb Dream-world of Global Hospitality. *Geoforum* 91: 170–181.

Rosenbush, Steve. 2014. Airbnb Says Data is 'Lifeblood' of Fast-Growing Business. *The Wall Street Journal*. https://www.wsj.com/articles/BL-CIOB-4115.

Siddiqui, Faiz. 2019. Internal Data Shows Uber's Reputation Hasn't Changed Much Since #DeleteUber. *The Washington Post*. https://www.washingtonpost.com/technology/2019/08/29/even-after-ubers-ipo-long-shadow-deleteuber-still-looms/.

Sweney, Mark. 2022. Airbnb Suspends All Operations in Russia and Belarus. *The Guardian*. https://www.theguardian.com/technology/2022/mar/04/airbnb-suspends-all-operations-in-russia-and-belarus.

Tanga, Martina. 2017. This Day in History: March 31. *Italian Art Society*. Blog post. https://www.italianartsociety.org/2016/03/the-italian-contemporary-artist-pippa-bacca-officially-giuseppina-pasqualino-di-marineo-tragically-died-on-this-day-march-31-2008/.

Uber.com. 2022. *Uber Technologies Inc.*

Vincent, James. 2021. Uber's New Minimum Wage Policy in the UK Doesn't Meet the Law Say Case Claimants. *The Verge*. https://www.theverge.com/2021/3/17/22335554/ubers-uk-minimum-wage-decision-employee-rights-flouting-law.

Waschsmuth, David, and Alexander Weisler. 2018. Airbnb and the Rent Gap: Gentrification Through the Sharing Economy. *Environment and Planning A: Economy and Space* 50 (6). https://doi.org/10.1177/0308518X18778038.

Zelaya, Ian. 2020. Uber Urges Those Who Tolerate Racism to Delete the App. *AdWeek*. https://www.adweek.com/brand-marketing/uber-urges-those-who-tolerate-racism-to-delete-the-app/.

CHAPTER 5

Embodied Computing and the Digital Intimacy of Wearable Technologies

In early 2022, the new instalment of the *Sex and the City* franchise—*And Just Like That*—set viewers and social media alight when it chose to depict an intimate moment between Charlotte and her husband, Harry. The scene—awkwardly interrupted by their young daughter caused quite a reaction for choosing to show Harry in what cinema audiences often refer to as "full frontal." Yet the scene conjured up another interesting moment when conversation turned not to what was beneath Harry's belt, but rather to what was on his finger. Indeed, in response to the death of their close friend, "Big," who suffered a heart attack while taking a virtual Peloton class,[1] this scene finds Charlotte trying to persuade Harry to wear the new Ōura ring—a so-called smart ring marketed primarily for sleep and fitness, among other health functions. For Charlotte, the ring's claim to monitor heart rate might just save Harry from the same fate as Big. The

---

[1] For those unfamiliar with the series, this new reboot of *Sex and the City* shows central protagonist Carrie Bradshaw living in mostly idyllic and high-end style on New York's Upper East Side, with her "on-again, off-again" love "Mr. Big" (or, John James Preston, played by Chris Noth). Firmly "on" and happily married, the pair discuss their upcoming trip to the Hamptons, which is delayed so Carrie can attend a piano recital. While she is out, Big suffers a heart attack following a Peloton ride and dies in the shower, just as Carrie arrives home. It is a scene that would be tragic were it not for the real-life reveals about Chris Noth's off-screen behaviour and accusations of sexual assault that surfaced just while the show was in production and no doubt contributed to his character's early demise. (Horton 2021).

---

product placement here is subtle but says much about the critical intersections between neoliberal fitness, data surveillance, gendered biometrics, and the strange forms of intimacy and hospitality that operate in wearable technologies, not to mention reinforcing a discourse of medical inaccuracy within wearable tech that assumes a smart ring might save someone from a heart attack.

Ōura of course, while slyly embedded into a new cultural entertainment product here, is not the only device of its kind. Other examples on (or soon to be on) the market include designs by Circular, BodiMetrics, Movano, and ArcX (Allenby 2022). Yet Finland-based Ōura is certainly the most stylish. With a sleek design, water resistance, multiple finish options, and an easy-to-wear structure, Ōura is compatible with both the Fitbit and Apple Watch and retails for approximately 300 USD. While the smart ring industry is admittedly still in its infancy and is being hailed as a more convenient alternative to wrist-worn smart devices, reviews are already mixed. A recent Instagram campaign for Ōura's Third Generation ring reveals the complicated relationship not only between consumers and new technologies, but between those technologies and bodies themselves. One particular post features a selection of rings in various finishes, all perched atop grey slate pillars with a similarly grey background. The metallic, rock, and modern aesthetic, combined with the absence of people in the post's imagery give the campaign an almost otherworldly or even alien feel. The caption reads, "Introducing our Ōura Gen3 Horizon: Also available in Rose Gold. Discover more about the new sleek, uninterrupted design with the link in our bio" (Ōura, Instagram, 2022).

While some of the 307 comments (as of October 2022) beneath the post are positive—using phrases such as "love it!" and "so cool!" and liberally employing the heart, clap, or fire emojis, the bulk of the comments are more critical. In particular, dozens of existing customers express dissatisfaction at having just recently purchased the previous version before the Gen3 was released and inquire about the procedure for return or upgrade. Other comments press for an explanation on the increased cost, particularly for the Rose Gold version. As one user writes: "PINK PREMIUM!?³? [sic] Why is the rose gold so much more expensive than the other colour ways in Horizon!? Aren't we done with sexist pricing?" (Ōura, Instagram, 2022). Another reads "I am disappointed in this brand. Newsom [the Governor of California] just got rid of the Pink Tax in CA but I guess Ōura missed the memo" (Ōura, Instagram, 2022). Along the same lines, a third comment adds: "Talk about a pink tax. I thought you partnered with natural cycles to empower women's health..." (Ōura, Instagram 2022). Gender-inflated pricing is not the only concern on Ōura's social media platform. Indeed, a separate comment thread on the same post raises concerns over data privacy. One expresses:

> Forcing people to pay a monthly membership to get their data is not fair at all. The ring is already expensive and its purpose is to collect data. I feel like when we buy a product that is made to collect data we should be able to access the data. I'm pretty sure that could be valid in court. @ouraring this might seriously backfire. (Ōura, Instagram, 2022)

Below this, another commenter asks, "[W]hy should we pay a monthly membership to access OUR OWN [sic] data???" (Ōura, Instagram, 2022). The two themes of critique that emerge here are fairly obvious and have much to do with how we think about future wearable technologies in the context of bodies (particularly gendered ones), the relationship between humans and machines, and the information such machines glean from our corporeal selves.

Smart rings are not the only example of this complex relationship, to be sure. Best represented by devices such as the Fitbit and the Apple Watch, wearable technologies have been a part of our daily lives and routines for some time now, with Apple recently releasing its Eight Generation Watch, along with a new "Ultra" model. Beyond their symbolic function as a marker of wealth, health, and leisure, the knowledge produced by these devices allows us to experience technology at the level of the body in a way that seems safe, intimate, helpful, and easy to understand. Virtual or not, the process still connects deeply to our biology and we *feel* it working. Wearable tech allows us to feel at ease in a sea of devices managing our schedules, our music, our spending practices, our data storage, and our surveillance. In comparison, Fitbit and the Apple Watch seem small and convenient—even more so in the case of the Ōura ring. They produce a knowledge of what is referred to as the Quantified Self[2] that is equal parts reassuring and alarming, using the familiarity and comfort of the body

---

[2] Quantified self refers both to the cultural phenomenon of self-tracking with technology and to a community of users and makers of self-tracking tools who share an interest in self-knowledge through numbers. Quantified self-practices overlap with the practice of lifelogging and other trends that incorporate technology and data acquisition into daily life, often with the goal of improving physical, mental, and/or emotional performances (see Lupton 2016).

itself to assuage fears about the digital unknown. As Hub Zwart (2017) puts it, we are "vulnerable and fragile beings, saved by, but also irrevocably infected by technology."

With smart rings and watches in mind then, this chapter considers the strange and the familiar, and the intimate forms of hospitality exposed through the proliferation of wearable technologies, within the larger context of digital health products that are primarily marketed towards women—and within an industry colloquially known as "FemTech." In what follows I offer a brief overview of women's digital health and its relationship to touch, intimacy, and hospitality. I then explore how the kinds of touch involved in biometric devices operate on the threshold of the foreign and familiar, occupying what robotics professor Masahiro Mori calls the "uncanny valley."[3] What is particularly interesting in the context of wearables is how we come to know our own bodies, even their most intimate and carnal functions, by the manipulation of our interiority into a data set, where interpretations and recommendations are determined in virtual space then beamed back to the body to be implemented. Or, in some cases even *implanted*. To offer a theory of hospitality in wearable technology I will work through a series of examples that expose the role of touch in the procurement of intimate data, and further link hospitality to discourses of gender and perfection, as well as biometric surveillance. While the wide range of biometric technologies as a whole is useful for thinking about how hospitality can be reimagined for a digital and posthuman future, it is particularly through the lens of gendered biometrics that discourses of self and other, as well as surveillance, are exacerbated. Ultimately, thinking about the extent to which digital replicas and prostheses offer alternating affects of comfort or uncertainty raises a number of serious questions for theories of strangeness so crucial to hospitality as our own bodies, through data, are made strangers to us.

FemTech, the World of Wearables and Digital Health

In order, however, to think through the gendered (in)hospitality of wearable biometrics, the wider range of health and fitness technologies marketed to women must be explored. Indeed, fitness tracking is often viewed

[3] In that the replica does not provide an apt replacement but rather produces a sense of uncertainty, a "dip" in the user's comfort and attachment to the digital product.

as a gender-neutral category, eliding the ways in which marketing and investment strategies subscribe to normative frameworks of race, class, and gender, as well as reproducing latent regimes of intersectional surveillance as well. In many ways both gender *and* race are curiously *erased* from most conversations around an industry dominated by players such as Fitbit and the Apple Watch, even as it is raced and gendered bodies that disproportionately come to be scrutinized and tracked, not to mention fall short of a series of metrics that use a white, middle-class, cis-gendered, heterosexual, reproductive, and abled body as a baseline for research and innovation. The parallels with more problematic forms of hospitality should be well-apparent here. As the other chapters in this volume explore, the project of hospitality itself is one in which women, people of colour, and the non-human or more-than-human both serve and suffer in unique but often invisible ways. Thinking about hospitality through the lens of digital products marketed to women in a self-monitoring capacity thus also reminds us of the stakes at play in reimagining ethics of welcome in a world where women's health and bodies have always been seen as strange.

In 2016, Ida Tin, the founder of the digital Danish menstruation application *Clue*, coined the term "FemTech" (Dodgson 2020), a portmanteau of "feminine" and "technologies" that refers to the wide range of digital products designed with women's health in mind. Due to the growing need for self-monitoring tracing in healthcare generally, the FemTech ecosystem is accelerating at a rapid pace, but is often approached without much critical attention to issues such as equitable access, data privacy, quality thresholds, and the taken-for-granted intimacy of expanding human-computer relationships (HCI) (see Diaz 2020; FemTech Collective 2021; Lupton 2016; Balfour Forthcoming). While the most utilized and profitable FemTech products include software and hardware such as ovulation and fitness trackers, as well as reproductive technologies, this only represents a fraction of health concerns affecting women. Moreover, although the availability of FemTech has been increasing over the last decade, the COVID-19 pandemic has accelerated the need for discreet, portable, and accessible digital tools that can be used in a self-monitoring capacity when access to face-to-face healthcare has been limited. Yet while COVID-19 has facilitated the growth of FemTech, it has also exacerbated and exposed significant gaps in the industry and its products, ranging from inconsistent policies and regulatory frameworks to concerns around quality control and data privacy (Lupton 2016; Rosas 2019; Heywood 2021), and a void of humanities research and theorization of emerging markets

(FemTech Analytics 2021). Perhaps the most glaring omission is the failure of mainstream FemTech to think beyond the (predominantly), white, cis-gendered, middle-class, abled body, not to mention a lack of consideration for women's bodies beyond their reproductive capabilities (Plan International 2021; Figueroa 2021). As such, FemTech is an industry simultaneously on the brink of advanced biometric technology and in serious need of reflection. Yet it is also an occasion to interrogate hospitality at the level of the body and its most intimate functions, highlighting the poignancy and permeability of the body as a threshold for hospitality and relations between selves and strangers.

Indeed, while FemTech is a rapidly evolving and expanding global market, there remains very little feminist research into the relationship between FemTech and the social construction of bodies, or into the link between bodies, data, and self-management—or what this chapter views as self-*estrangement*. In academic literature, for example, little attention is given to how forms of marginalization intersect but are overlooked in products that largely assume a white, heterosexual, affluent, childbearing, and able-bodied user (Corbin 2020). Moreover, many LGBTQIA users do not identify with the "Fem" prefix on their digital healthcare products (Serrano 2007; Alloy 2021). The emphasis on particular bodies here is crucial when thinking about the forms of biometric discipline and surveillance that operate in self-monitoring technologies. These "strange" functions and the data produced by them are rarely scrutinized, not rigorously tested, often not medically accurate, and do not capture the diversity of women's experience despite purporting to transmit knowledge about the body back to users. The result here is a narrative of perfection that can only be achieved through a disciplinary regime that aims to improve, manage, and, ultimately, make those strange bodies more familiar.

Furthermore, the wearables industry as a whole assumes a male user, first and foremost, with specific applications for those who identify as women developed as an afterthought. Despite the fresh innovations of the market, and excitement over its potential, biometric wearables very much mimic the research trajectories of the healthcare industry in general, indicative of what many scholars refer to as the "gender data gap" (see Criado-Perez 2019; Buvinic and Levine 2016). In Spring 2021, for instance, the UK government launched a "Call for Evidence" for a new digital strategy for women's health, arguing: "For generations, women have lived with a health and care system that is mostly designed by men, for men. This has meant that not enough is known about conditions that only affect women, or about how conditions that affect both men and women impact women in different ways" (Thomas 2021). But this is not just an issue in England and Europe. In the US, for instance, women of childbearing age were effectively "banned" from participating in clinical trials for decades—an omission that was only reversed in the 1990s (FemTech Analytics 2021). Much like the lag time between the development of men's and women's contraception (i.e. the condom and "the pill"),[4] wearables that specifically capture the experiences of those who identify as women do not have the infrastructure, capital, or critical research as do products developed for the men's or "gender neutral" market. Even those women who identify within normative frameworks of gender are still rarely involved at higher levels of design, investment, or consultation when it comes to the digital products paradoxically designed for them. Indeed, the estrangement here is clear— not only are women's health issues seen as "strange" within a patriarchal health imaginary but the tools developed for women (i.e. wearable technologies) are designed with the direct intention of managing such strangeness. Wearable or "embodied" technologies (see Pedersen and Iliadis 2020) thus operate on a threshold between the familiar and foreign, where the body itself becomes a platform for knowledge. And, as products that simultaneously require intimate access and produce intimate results, wearable technologies should be both desired and feared. Moreover, they continue to expose the relations of hospitality to be complex and unstable beginning with the very first moment they meet the body.

Intersectionality (or Lack Thereof) in Fitness Tracking

As the development of FemTech demonstrates, thinking through intimate forms of wearable tech takes on even more significant resonance when viewed through the lens of gender and the particular forms of biotracking that manage women's bodies. Here, wearable technologies mimic culture and prove not so new after all—that is to say: women have *always* been taught to feel estranged from their own bodies. This is likely no more obvious and fascinating than in the vast promises of the FemTech industry, where wearable devices have emerged to help "women" (still a broad

---

[4] Let us also not forget that the drug Viagra was initially found to alleviate period pain in early trials. This research into the benefits of Viagra for those who menstruate was dropped once it was also found to help treat erectile dysfunction (see Reid 2019).

categorization used unproblematically by most in the wearables industry)[5] manage their fitness, reproductive health, sex lives, and even their safety. Perhaps the most well-known of these products—precursors to tools such as the Ōura ring—are the ovulation trackers developed for both Fitbit and Apple Watch (among many other "smart" brands). Designed to augment the knowledge women have had about their own biological processes from the beginning of humankind, these particular devices monitor, among other metrics, length of cycle, flow, and fertility levels. No longer an afterthought, the wearables industry has shifted from promoting a gender-neutral product to highlighting gender-specific tools as part of its marketing strategy. In recent web ads for the Series 8 Apple Watch, its FemTech-related functions received top billing. Scrolling through the initial series of watch images on the Apple Watch landing site, one settles quickly on the text: "Your essential companion is now even more powerful. Introducing temperature sensing for deeper insights into women's health" (Apple 2022). A footnote directs visitors to the "Health" section of the webpage, where more users can access more information on the cycle tracking, period predictions, and related ovulatory data that can be gleaned from Apple's latest wearable. Significantly, promoting the new Series 8 watch as an "essential companion" not only firmly locates women's health and fitness within a network of social relations, but also makes the device itself part of that sociality. Indeed, it is hard not to think of Haraway's notion of "companion species" (2003) here, described by Lupton (2016) as relationships where both parties learn from and engage one another, as a form of "co-evolving." For Lupton, the companion species trope acknowledges "the liveliness of digital data and the relational nature of our interaction with these data" (2016). The temptation, and indeed the *tendency*, to read these devices as new useful tools is clear, yet

---

[5] I use "women" here to designate a particular language used by those who design and market biometric tracking products and do so with a recognition of the ways in which such a category glosses over the diverse experiences and identities of those who menstruate. This chapter has much to say about intersectional marginalization within wearable tech but it is worth acknowledgement here right away. These assumptions that the industry and even the medical field make around what constitutes a woman (i.e. having a uterus and able to biologically reproduce) elide the multiple forms of oppression and exclusion faced by non-binary, trans, and other queer or non-confirming bodies who may menstruate but *not* identify as women and vice versa. See Caroline Colvin's (2021) essay for *Health.com* for a critical narrative of non-binary menstruation and discussion of how transphobia and period stigma are linked in dominant health discourse.

as Cornell University's Karen Levy cautions, there are many other operations at play in the collection and interpretation of intimate data generated by devices such as the Apple Watch. As Levy warns, "the act of measurement is not neutral...every technology of measurement and classification legitimates certain forms of knowledge and experience, while rendering others invisible" (in Tiffany 2018). While the concerns over how private information from menstruation and ovulation trackers is (increasingly) well-documented by myself and others,[6] I want to be clear about my focus here. These forms of "knowledge and experience" are, at their very core, connected to a discourse of otherness and (self) estrangement that position women's bodies not only as strange but also as unintelligible *to themselves*.

The assumption here is that women can't seem to manage their own menstruation—a point that Dr Katherine White, Assistant Professor of Obstetrics and Gynaecology at Boston University, confirms. As an advisor to Fitbit's ovulation app, White suggests that "women have a hard time remembering all the nuances from cycle to cycle, how long or the timing of various symptoms," and that she asks women every day "'when was your last period?' but it's seldom that patients can answer off the top of their head" (in Lovett 2018). A similar assumption can be read in a different kind of wearable product, one that offers an update on the traditional sports bra. "Smart" high-performance apparel brand Sensilk launched its Fight Tech Bra in May 2015, which uses sensors embedded in the undergarment to measure biometric data such as heart rate, respiratory rate, and calories burned during a workout (Hill 2015). Yet when the product was

[6] In early Summer 2022, FemTech made the global news for all the wrong reasons. On Friday, 24 June 2022, the US Supreme court officially overturned Roe vs. Wade, the landmark 1973 ruling that established a constitutional right to abortion, leaving such matters now to individual states to decide. Following the decision of the Supreme Court, and over the summer of 2022, news and social media were flooded with calls for women to delete their menstruation, ovulation, or pregnancy apps based on the fear that the data generated from these apps will not only be sold to third-party advertisers, but possibly accessed by enforcement agencies or even subpoenaed to prosecute those seeking now-outlawed forms of reproductive care. These fears are not unfounded—in December 2018, for instance, London-based charity Privacy International reported that many well-known menstruation apps were regularly sharing user data with social media channels. Of the 36 applications they tested, more than 61% immediately transferred data to Facebook when a user opened the app. This is not just a challenge for start-ups. Indeed, recently the ovulation app *Flo* reached a settlement with the Federal Trade Commission after allowing the data accumulated by its almost 100 million users to be shared with third-party companies, including advertisers (Singer 2021).

launched, all of the media focus was on its designer, CEO Donald Yang, who promoted the sports bra with the promise that "we analyze all this information and give the woman a fitness goal" (in Murray 2015). The irony here should be clear: not only are women rarely involved in the aesthetic or functional design of a garment made precisely for them, but they are also not involved in the interpretation of the data that garment generates. Sensilk's biometric tracker, as well as the ovulation and fertility functions on more conventional products such as the Apple Watch, reminds us that the majority of these devices are not only engineered and profited upon by men, but also targeted to women specifically through the capitalization of women's anxiety over their own bodies. The combination of feminine-coded design, images of fashionable and fit bodies, and biological tracking functionality work together to produce a narrative around women's bodies that follows along in a long line of advertising targeting women that suggests not only are we not in control of our own bodies, but that they can *and should* be improved—often at the hands or ingenuity of men. Rose gold, designer bands, and the promotion of fitness trackers that can take you from your yoga class through to date night are not inherently a negative development, but considering that in 2017 women held just 23% of Apple's technology jobs (Liedtke 2018), it is important to note that while purporting to help women regulate their own bodily functions, most of these applications are created by men reinforcing the binaries of strange and familiar and the desire to bring the strange (woman) into a regime of decipherability.

To be clear, this is as problematic with regard to race as it is with gender, and it is imperative to think of how both forms of marginalization intersect in biometric fitness. Thus, an intersectional and genealogical analysis of digital health fitness trackers, as forms of biometric surveillance, is crucial to both interpreting how gender, race, and class interact in the representation, design, and manufacturing of technological "solutions" in ways that productively overlap but remain distinct aspects of the experience of marginalization and estrangement that are critical components of the project of hospitality. Apple is no stranger to claims of racially biased biometrics within their hit wrist-worn product. While the original Apple Watch was an immediate hit when it was released in 2015, shortly after, customers began reporting on Reddit that they had a hard time activating the touch sensors on the underside of the watch if they had dark tattoos in that area. Of course, it wasn't just those with tattoos that were having trouble—people of colour also began reporting that the touch sensors would not "recognize" their skin. Apple, like many wearable manufacturers, uses sensors that beam green light towards the skin (Taylor 2015). Green light penetrates the skin just enough to get a reading without reaching too deep and faces less competition from other forms of light. This green light enters the first few layers of skin and measures the rate of blood flow beneath the surface. Green light, however, is more likely to be absorbed by the skin of people with higher melanin content *before* it can get a reading. The darker the skin (tattoo or otherwise), the less likely the sensors are to capture data when the person is moving. In other words, early versions of the Apple Watch failed to recognize some people of colour as *living human bodies*, an issue that was also a problem with Fit Bit (Hailu 2019; Wetsman 2022). I draw attention to this problem, not just to call out racial bias in fitness tracking sensors (inadvertent as it may be), but to recognize the ways in which race, and gender too, are simultaneously and paradoxically both highlighted but also made invisible by biometric tracking technologies. Whether denying access to a room via retina scan or to a feature of an app or device that requires touch ID, these forms of tracking seem to find certain biometric identities more strange than others, reminding us that hospitality is not only gendered but racialized as well. As a result, and according to Sanders, "the rise of wearable biometric technologies has significant implications for the augmentation and co-extension of biopower and patriarchal power" (2017). That this is accomplished through a reading that occurs through the skin, the body's largest organ. Skin is that which is permeable but also tough and brings the science and surveillance of biometrics into relation with intimate forms of welcome and estrangement or, we might say, flesh and code. For the technology here is not an evacuation of the flesh. Instead, it *relies* on it. As Wissinger notes, "the technoscientific dream of leaving the flesh behind, of turning the body into code, feeds all too easily into the idea of body as data, a slippery slope that leads to conceiving the body as pliable, manipulable, and fully controllable" (2017). Wissinger's caution is well-taken here; body-cum-data is indeed a dangerous trajectory that both elides the ethics (or violence) of touch and also suggests not only that the body is something distinct from technology, but that it loses agency in a relation we assume is always a one-way transaction. In what follows, I want to think of touch as a threshold of relationality rather than biometrics for identification. Indeed, skin can be simultaneously datafied and dermatological but also a membrane: a porous site where the encounter between self and other occurs, and as a locus of alternate hospitality and hostility.

CARNAL HOSPITALITY: WEARABLES AND THE FRONTIER
OF TOUCH

Perhaps the most intimate effect of wearable devices occurs through their use of and, indeed, their imperative, for touch. It is through touch that the device *reads* the body, through advanced sensory technologies that, depending on the brand and device, might include accelerometers (tracking movement in multiple directions), gyroscopes (to measure angle and rotation), altimeters (for altitude and pressure), temperature sensors and bioimpedance sensors (to collect data for heart rate), and optical sensors (using light to measure pulse) (see Lashkari 2019; Henriksen et al. 2018; Abt et al. 2017; Hayes 2014). According to Apple, these sensors (most, if not all of which are available in Series 6 or newer models) can monitor mobility and cardio fitness, fall detection, medical information storage, blood oxygen levels, irregular heart rhythms, and ECG readings (Apple 2022). As Apple promotes on its "Health" site, "the future of healthcare is in your hands...The result is care that becomes more efficient, more personalised and ultimately *more human*" (Apple 2022, my emphasis). Similarly, in a blog post on how to use a Garmin watch to its fullest health-tracking potential, the company concludes, "Your wearable can be with you every step of the way when you're keeping a close eye on your health" (Garmin 2022). In both of these examples, the individualization, responsibilization, and, importantly, the *anthropomorphism* of health emerge as normative themes within the fitness tracking industry. These themes also serve to reinforce and enhance one another. The individual responsibilization of fitness not only fulfils a neoliberal strategy of making docile and disciplined citizens (this time through fitness rather than the surveillance tactics of Uber and Airbnb as discussed in Chap. 4); it also subscribes to a tool-using paradigm in which the device itself is mobilized in the service of *human* advancement. Touch technology thus becomes a mechanism for human growth and improvement, rather than a relational figure that might allow us to conceptualize our interactions with fitness trackers as hospitable in any way.

These discourses of self-monitoring and improvement also reinforce the notion of the stranger by suggesting that, in spite of the anthropomorphic emphasis of fitness tracking, human bodies are ultimately deficient or lacking in some way. That is to say, they are "out of sync" with themselves—almost explicitly demonstrating the messages of self-estrangement that this chapter aims to unpack. Indeed, in another example of the growing smart ring industry, the company Movano promotes its health tracking capabilities with a particularly apt by-line, asking prospective consumers, "How long has it been since you felt like *you*? If you've been out of touch with your body for a while, allow us to re-introduce you" (Movano 2022). Here Movano capitalizes on a narrative of identity crisis already popular in the marketing of fitness products, while at the same time highlighting this crisis as affective, intimate, and deeply connected to the ways in which identity is constructed through the body's relationship with external forces and indeed, its relationship with itself. Information about the body in this case—and by extension of the self and its capacity for improvement and knowledge—is gleaned through the sensors that use human skin as an interface in such a way that two independent forces (the body and the technology) *touch* one another. It is here that Mori's "uncanny valley" emerges once more to reveal just how close the foreign and familiar are in the particularities of touch that surround wearable trackers. In a business article written for LinkedIn's Pulse platform, Muneeb Bokhari describes this "almost but not quite" phenomenon of the uncanny valley with regard to the Apple Watch. He argues that "wearables occupy a space between utility and the self that many are not particularly comfortable with…if your wrist tingles, you look down because it's either someone shaking you or your digital appendage is demanding attention" (2015). In most cases, the uncanny is used to describe a scenario where a non-human object or being demonstrates human resemblance—the "valley" here is the moment our affinity for such beings "dips" as they reveal themselves to be not human at all. For Mori, "the sense of eeriness [produced by this dip in affinity] is probably a form of instinct that protects us from proximal, rather than distal, sources of danger" (1970, 2012). Mori's definition, while a groundbreaking insight into the world of robotics, does not necessarily take into account the relationship between humans and wearable technology that is, at its core, proximal to the point of being penetrative. Unlike the unsettling closeness brought by the android figure, for example, whose resemblance to the human produces the uncanny effects, the effects in this case are produced within the human body itself. In other words, it is not the technology of the wearable that becomes strange; instead, it *makes the body strange*. Therefore, thinking about the extent to which digital replicas and prostheses offer affects of simultaneous comfort and uncertainty disrupts the taken-for-granted utility of wearable tech and raises a number of serious questions for theories of hospitality. How is it, for instance, that touch, as a sense, can be both comfortable, familiar, and *homely*, while at the same time unfamiliar, strange, unsettling, and uncanny? Touch is a sense we employ often without thinking and its benign role as a threshold or boundary between the internal and external is rarely questioned. We might think of the newer models of mobile phones here—those that require touch identification to access the device—and the regularity with which the human and machine meet this threshold. Beyond that, we might think of that moment of touch as alternately hospitable or hostile as the user takes up the role of guests who must (biometrically) identify themselves before they are welcomed. Touch ID acts as a barrier to absolute hospitality, to be sure, denying any stranger access unless they can (correctly) identify themselves. This feature thus reminds us of the central paradox of ethics of welcome that has been raised several times in this volume. Indeed, what is imperative for security, and the protection of information and private data, is problematic for hospitality as an unconditional set of ethics.

So how are the touch technologies of wearable tech both a source of familiarity and foreignness? Just like sensory human touch can be both a source of pain and pleasure, this sublimity[7] is amplified in the touch of the wearable device first and foremost because of the effects of the uncanny, or what Zwart (2017) calls the "too biocompatible" or "too real" closeness of the device. In the case of wearables, the closeness is not just in skin contact, but in touching the most intimate processes our body undertakes—sleep, BMI, hydration, menstruation—all that which happens not just on the surface of the flesh but beneath it. Skin is what connects us to the world around us, through which we experience our surroundings but also that which registers harm and alerts us to danger. As the philosopher Edward Casey elaborates, "it is on this surface that the depths come to expression, thus to our notice; but the same skin surface, precisely because of its acute sensitiveness, is vulnerable to exploitation by others—to their unwanted incursion in situations of trauma or torture" (2015). It is a border agent, protective but porous, delimiting but vulnerable. Skin is also what we call the thin after-market membranes that we purchase to protect our digital devices.

---

[7] I take Burke's definition here—the dual emotional quality of fear and attraction—to highlight the ways in which wearable technologies offer a sense of awe produced by the intermingling of philia and phobia in the technological object (see Edmund Burke's *A Philosophical Enquiry into the Origin of Our Ideas of the Sublime and Beautiful*, 1757).

While speaking on the hospitality of language—what he calls "linguistic hospitality" that is exercised through the process of translation—Richard Kearney (2019) suggests that "we can find ourselves aliens within our own langue *maternelle* and within the depths of our own minds." The truest translations, according to Kearney, are those that allow that strange and unfamiliar text to retain its strangeness—a translation that makes a text newly intelligible but does not subsume its otherness into a regime of complete understanding. Might we think of the act of touch in wearables as a form of translation? The host and guest languages—or the transformation from bodies to data—as a form of hospitality possibilized by touch and the sensor? As Kearney illustrates—some of the greatest moments of hospitality that have occurred throughout history and antiquity have been moments of touch (though certainly not without violence): fists turned to handshakes, hands transforming food from flour to bread to serve guests—not to mention the Christian narratives about the healing touch of Christ (Kearney 2019). These narratives remind us that hospitality is, first and foremost, and for better or worse, *carnal*—a word often misrepresented as a reference to sexual relations when, in actuality, "carnal" derives from Latin etymology relating to the English word "meat" or "flesh" (Merriam Webster 2022a). Outside of the Latin, the "carnal" has been adopted in religion and moral philosophy to pertain to "things of the flesh," juxtaposed of course against the "things of the Spirit" (Romans 8:5–6, KJV). It is an interesting paradox, if we follow Kearney's insistence that these forms of human intimacy, including eating, translate the self to the other, and vice versa, through touch. Indeed, these same touches have often been relegated to the sacrilege, the carnal, and the immoral. In these dualisms the physical, corporeal, or animal is both worldly and ephemeral, compared to the divine and eternal spiritual realm.

I want to suggest that it is hospitality, particularly through wearable technology, that disrupts this binary. As an ethic that demands intimacy, touch, and possibly violence, hospitality is simultaneously worldly and embodied but also, in its most absolute forms, irrevocably divine. It is a sacred opening to the other, human, or more-than-human. In Kearney's words "carnal hospitality can operate at several levels of embodied exchange, but it is in touch that the most basic act of exposure to others occurs" (2019). In the context of fitness tracking and wearable technologies, we can think of touch as an act of exposure but also an act of knowledge. Exposure is in the *knowing* of the other—here generated through the transfer of data via sensors. Yet hospitality also fails in this context and not only because of the ease with which it settles into surveillance, patriarchy, and capitalism. As Kearney describes, there is only hospitality when there is the "'double sensation' of touch—a phenomenon of reversibility where touching is also a being touched" (Kearney 2019). There is no doubt that a wearable fitness tracker touches us, but can we touch it in return? Are these technologies "touched" by their wearer? Ultimately, touch offers not so much a foreclosure of hospitality but an invitation to determine the hospitable touch from the hostile one. Indeed, Kearney suggests, there is "a hermeneutic *responsibility* to discern between handshakes—those that express genuine hospitality and those that mask hostility" (2019, my emphasis). Perhaps wearables offer something different to this process of discernment. If we think beyond the handshake as a symbolic (and anthropomorphic) gesture of welcome, what does the more-than-human potential of touch technologies possibly teach us about how to welcome other forms of sensory encounter or, at the very least, offer an invitation to touch back?

Strange Selves and Excarnation in Wearable Technologies

Whether through the non-reciprocal and intimate act of touching, or the gendered and racialized relationship between embodiment, data, and surveillance, there is no doubt that wearable technologies produce a knowledge about the body that is paradoxically estranged from the body itself. Wearable devices shift the relationship between self and other by taking over the host function from the body, not only acting as an external repository for the body's data but guiding us through its interpretation. Through these devices, we are turned inside out, and that which we used to call familiar and homely—food and drink, sleep, speech and heart rate, and more—is no longer ours. It is external to us (*even if implanted within our own bodies*), datafied, and governed. It doesn't just reveal our desires; it gives us new ones by way of targeted step counts and recommended calorie intake and uncovers what's beneath the surface of our skin.

How then, might we read the excarnation of digital technology as a kind of estrangement, but one brought back to the body as an unfamiliar metric, making us—in Kristeva's words—strangers to ourselves? Kristeva writes: "The foreigner comes in when the consciousness of my difference arises, and he disappears when we all acknowledge ourselves as foreigners, unamenable to bonds and communities" (1991). Thinking about this movement from familiarity to difference in the encounter with wearable trackers offers an interesting revision of Kristeva's thoughts, for as she suggests, such strangeness is ameliorated not through a reconciliation of difference (by way of biometrics, fitness goals, and self-knowledge) but a welcome of difference that acknowledges the ways in which we are all strange—technologies too. But what do we do with the space in between; this space where carnal and code, body, and bot converge in a way that conjures Freud's *unheimlich* and renders the foreign familiar, and the familiar strange? Self-estrangement also returns us to the uncanny, again, that which produces an "affective experience of the uncontrollable responses of our own internal drives" (in Ravetto-Biagioli 2019). We might clarify this further as the *digital* uncanny, which mimics the human—its gestures, actions, even emotions, and relationships—through non-human technologies such as surveillance, collated data, predictive algorithms, and the digital body management systems explored in this chapter. The uncanny affect here is that we are becoming more like machines and machines more like us. It is through Freud's interpretation of this story in his essay *The Uncanny* that we are given language to understand this phenomenon—what he terms the *heimlich* and *unheimlich*, a parasitical word pair in which the familiar always carries the anticipation of its phantom other—the strange. In David Simpson's words, "what is unheimlich is also, at the same time, heimlich...[The terms] are bound together etymologically as codependent and perhaps even interchangeable: every host is a guest in the making, every stranger is familiar" (2013). Here, Simpson gestures to the central problem of hospitality as well as its paradox. There is no hospitality without its other; host and guest are, in other words and to recall Haraway once more, companion species—interreliant, symbiotic, parasitical, and marsupial.

And so, we cannot actually distinguish between the familiar and foreign in these wearable devices. They are strange in their closeness, not in their distance. A closeness that in psychoanalytic terms was once familiar but from which we have become estranged. Our own bodies, through data, made strangers to us. Again, following Freud, these unsettling intimacies—private bio-systems, secrets buried beneath the flesh, and perhaps, in his words, repressed desires—are those which were meant to stay hidden and are now exposed. They disturb the boundary between exposed and hidden, artificial and natural, and that which we would have ordinarily rendered non-human and perhaps abject. Much like the automaton

Olimpia in Hoffman's gothic horror tale *Der Sandman*, or we might say Samantha in the 2016 film, *Her*[8]—the problem is not that machine knows us; it is that it knows us better than we know ourselves. The implications of wearables are of course far more than the philosophical. Even as they get under our skin in an uncanny way, they also project what is internal back to ourselves as a form of knowledge, giving us a bird's-eye view of our own corporeal strengths and limits. With wearables we are rendered transparent but also made into Gods. With wearables it is possible to see the data and *be* the data at the same time.

In an article entitled "The Data Driven Life," published in *The New York Times Sunday Magazine* in 2010, before the release of either Fitbit or the Apple Watch, Gary Wolf suggested that these forms of data can serve as a tool for "introspection," a reflection of ourselves, made possible by the digital through which we glimpse and learn new things about ourselves. According to Natasha Schüll, for Wolf "tracking tools become ethical tools, technologies of the self…a pathway from self-knowledge to self-transformation" (2016). But it is an unsettling and incomplete transformation. As Ravetto-Biagioli argues, "[t]hese multifaceted images neither present us with any experience of otherness that would help us ground ourselves nor offer us a unified image of ourselves that we can identify with as a subject" (2019). These are no ordinary tools in other words; they are both prosthetic and penetrative, attached to our bodies as an appendage but also embedded as they pierce our corporeal surface and again conjure that uncanny valley between human and non-human, organic, and artificial.

Ultimately, wearable gadgets function as a form of what Kearney calls "excarnation," whereby the body no longer registers, through our own interpretation, how we "feel" but how the machine feels us. We might think of this estrangement as "a question of shifting the relations from subject, citizen, or autonomous individual to user, participant, follower, and ultimately the self—one that is not a product of life experience but a role (or game skin, the changeable attributes of one's online avatar or game persona) you step into" (Ravetto-Biagioli 2019). In other words, we adopt the identity given to us by the data—an easy task when according to companies such as Fitbit, there is "something for everyone" (Fitbit 2022). Interesting, the names given to Fitbit's tracking models seem to capture the persona of their ideal user. Depending on the "role" one steps into, they might identify with any number of Fitbit's labels including "Charge,"

---

[8] See Chap. 3 of this volume.

"Luxe," "Inspire," or "Ace." Fitbit also offers a quiz to help determine which tracker is "right for you." In a way, wearable trackers offer a kind of digital makeover, providing pathways to body optimization but also producing a new technological subject. As Sanders (2017) describes, "both because they understand they may be observed externally at any time and because they may understand self-tracking as a mode of personal agency, [users of] self-trackers will assume, with increasing vigilance and precision, the job of policing themselves." In this way the task of excarnation is not even accomplished by the device itself but, rather by the user who consents, however tacitly, to the tracking regimes that render them foreign and suspicious. Under the guise of digital agency, the work of estrangement and discipline is given back to the body in such a way that such bodies do not suffer self-estrangement but actively participate in their own.

Conclusion: Hospitality and (the) Posthuman Touch

The 1-minute and 15-second advertisement on UltraHuman's Kickstarter page opens with a blurry shot of a dark room with a floor-to-ceiling illuminated screen. As the camera pans in, a shadowy figure walks into the frame from behind the screen. The figure is reminiscent of an android or biomechanical being of some kind. It is only a silhouette but recalls the wiry tendons and metal joints of a robotic exoskeleton without its synthetic skin. A voice soon speaks: "Biowearables are evolving our definition of human health" suggesting that this figure may be the future of such evolution (UltraHuman 2022b). Before the figure steps into focus, however, the scene changes to show a human hand against a stark white background as the voice introduces the focus of the Kickstarter campaign: a "revolutionary metabolism tracking ring" (UltraHuman 2022b). The human hand wears this ring on the index finger, amidst a series of distinct tattoos. What follows is a sequence of bodies engaging in sport and depicted in a kaleidoscope-style video. They are, to be fair, conventionally "fit" bodies but still somewhat diverse, ranging from East and South Asian to Black, Mixed Race, and Indigenous. According to this video and the adjacent Kickstarter website, the UltraHuman ring promises to help users "decode" their metabolism with indexing for movement, sleep, heart rate, body temperature, and more. To be sure, this is not a scheme without a price tag and is still nestled firmly within the fitness tracking industry. But I want to suggest that we can also read the UltraHuman ring beyond its conventional use of biometric technologies to see how there are things happening beneath the surface, between the lines, or under the skin, that offer a new way of thinking hospitality—perhaps even *decoding* it—and keeps the digital future of hospitality alive.

I am thinking in particular of the curious choice of language the ring employs to distinguish itself from competitors. Indeed, both the notion of an "ultra" human and the explicit Kickstarter invitation extends to bio-hackers conjure figures that are critical for rethinking the laws of hospitality in order that it might continue to operate in the context of our inevitable digital future. And so to conclude this chapter, I offer some thoughts on the "ultra" human as a figure of ethical potential that displaces some of the surveillance and excarnation of the mainstream fitness tracking industry before exploring the concept of hacking in detail as a conclusion to this volume. As a way of reading the UltraHuman smart ring as a wearable tracker that (perhaps inadvertently) displaces the human as the primary ethical subject, I would like to consider "ultra" here as a possible synonym for the "post" prefix that liberates ethics of hospitality from its anthropomorphic social boundaries and philosophical assumptions. I use posthuman here therefore to designate both the notion of a "future" and technologically modified human but also the rejection of humanism and turn away from traditional humanist thought and experience. In doing so, I draw on a particular line of thought that moves beyond the human as a fixed or stable category of identity or, in the case of this book, a stable category of ethics. As Braidotti writes, "the posthuman predicament is such as to force a displacement of the lines of demarcation between structural differences, or ontological categories, for instance between the organic and the inorganic, the born and the manufactured, flesh and metal, electronic circuits and organic nervous systems" (2013). It is through this notion of the posthuman that we might begin to think about a project of hospitality that neither relies on its anthropomorphic roots nor takes for granted the category of human as the sole giver or receiver (host or guest) of ethical consideration. Doing so reconfigures the convergence of human and computer and the phobias associated with machine learning as something potentializing rather than something to be feared. Braidotti refers to this as the "becoming-machine axis," one that "cracks open the division between humans and technological circuits, introducing biotechnologically mediated relations as foundational for the constitution [of] the subject" (2013). Following Braidotti, rather than think about the uncanny effects of machines becoming like us, and vice versa, what if we were to rethink this relation, not as an estrangement from self but a reconfiguring of the self as relational and co-dependent rather than ontologically secure and separate? The UltraHuman thus alerts us to an entirely new possibility—that of a more-than-human ethics or ethics towards the more-than-human. As Braidotti cautions, "we assert our attachment to the species as if it were a matter of fact, a given. So much so that we construct a fundamental notion of rights around the Human...we need to devise new social, ethical, and discursive schemes of subject formation to match the profound transformations we are undergoing" (2013). What if hospitality offered this opportunity?

If it could, then, perhaps we could indeed "touch back." This may be easier theorized than actually achieved of course. For Claudia Castañeda (2001), "boundary-crossing does not in itself constitute an effective politics"; instead, the boundary-crossing of the cyborg or bionic being, as well as the technologies that predetermine such beings, must be thought of "in terms of how a particular body's matter and meaning work in and through each other: how the stuff of this body generates meanings, and how its meanings come to be materially embodied." In other words, the posthuman need not be in possession of a "skin" or kinetic fibres that connect to a thalamus—where information and sensory processing occurs in the brain—in order to touch and be touched. If we are able to think of touch and, indeed, of embodiment not as the proprietary material and sensory experience of the human but rather as an interconnected relationality to the world, then we might begin to think of not only a posthuman touch (and affect) but also a posthuman hospitality where we are brought into relation with, and touched by, diverse others. De-centring the human senses and the anthropomorphic body from relations of hospitality brings us back to an ethics that is not dependent on strict delineations of host and guest but a complex network of human and more-than-human actors that are both co-dependent and co-constitutive. In this way, according to Ahmed and Stacey (2001),

> 'my body' does not 'belong to me': embodiment is what opens out the intimacy of 'myself' with others. The relationship between bodies is characterised by a 'with' that precedes, or is the condition of possibility for, the apartness of 'my body'. This 'with' is the fleshiness of the world which inhabits us and is inhabited by us—flesh, not understood simply as matter, but as the very sensibility of the seen, and the very sight of the sensible.

This is not, to be sure, a way of discounting the lived and material experiences of hospitality and, particularly *in*hospitality, which we know have specific and differential consequences for the marginalized (whether human, animal, machine, or nature). It *is*, however, to suggest an alternative animation of hospitality—one rejected but also revived in the context of wearable touch technologies, and which retains a feminist politics of location without relying on a politics of humanism. In this framework touch, and hospitality itself, become in Kearney's words, a "matter of primal embodied wisdom operating in the three senses of *sense/sens*—sensation, orientation and meaning: three senses which mark every genuine encounter between self and stranger" (2019).

In a 2022 review of the UltraHuman ring, Natasha Lomas describes her "Four weeks as an UltraHuman 'Cyborg.'" Drawing on the familiar portmanteau of cybernetic and organism, Lomas suggests that "becoming a cyborg is no longer as sci-fi as that sounds" (2022b). While such a description recalls a now long-standing fascination with the bionic body—robotic prostheses, artificial, or synthetic organs, and 3D-printed heart valves, for instance—it also raises significant questions for the philosophy of hospitality. What would it mean to be embedded by a foreign other or object, to have it grow in and with your biological body, or sync up to your existing human nerves and tendons, even your brain? If absolute hospitality is modelled on the ethical incorporation of the other—particularly one that remains other—then the bionic or cyborg body seems to be emblematic of a posthuman revision of hospitality. In this way, the UltraHuman is indeed both post and more-*than*; not just an appendage whereby the boundaries of self and other, human, and machine are clearly demarcated, but an assemblage of human-computer processes, agencies, and identities. In other words, what if we started to think about such technologies not as separate from us, but as part of us, and us of them? Such a thinking untethers the dualities of self and other, guest and host, and radically reenergizes the possibility of *hacking* hospitality to recode our relations through and with digital strangers.

References

Abt, Gant, et al. 2017. The Validity and Inter-device Variability of the Apple Watch™ for Measuring Maximal Heart Rate. *Journal of Sports Sciences* 36 (13). https://doi.org/10.1080/02640414.2017.1397282.

Ahmed, Sara and Jackie Stacey. 2001. *Thinking Through the Skin*. Routledge.

Allenby, Charlie. 2022. 5 of the Best Smart Rings for Runners. *Runners World*. https://www.runnersworld.com/uk/gear/a40459007/best-smart-rings/.

Alloy, Dana. 2021. Embracing the 'Fem' in FemTech. *Inne.io* https://www.inne.io/en/blog/article/embracing-the-fem-in-femtech.

Apple Health. 2022. Apple.com. https://www.apple.com/uk/ios/health/.

Apple Series 8 Watch. 2022. Apple.com. https://www.apple.com/uk/apple-watch-series-8/.

Balfour, Lindsay, ed. 2023 (Forthcoming). *FemTech: Intersectional Interventions in Women's Digital Health*. Palgrave.

Bokhari, Muneeb. 2015. The Uncanny Valley of Wearables. *LinkedIn Pulse*. https://www.linkedin.com/pulse/uncanny-valley-wearables-muneeb-bokhari/.

Braidotti, Rosi. 2013. *The Posthuman*. Cambridge: Polity.

Buvinic, Mayra, and Ruth Levine. 2016. Closing the Gender Data Gap. *Significance* 13 (2). https://doi.org/10.1111/j.1740-9713.2016.00899.x.

Casey, Edward. 2015. "Skin Deep" Bodies Edging into Place. In *Carnal Hermeneutics*, ed. Richard Kearney and Brian Treanor. Fordham UP.

Castañeda, Claudia. 2001. Robotic Touch. In *Thinking Through the Skin*, Eds. Sara Ahmed and Jackie Stacey. Routledge.

Colvin, Caroline. 2021. What it's Like to Have a Period as a Non-Binary Person: 'We Need to Stop Associating Periods with Womanhood.' *Health.com*. https://www.health.com/mind-body/lgbtq-health/menstruating-as-non-binary-person.

Corbin, Bethany. 2020. Digital Micro-Aggressions and Discrimination: FemTech and the 'Othering' of Women. *Nova Law Review* 44: 1–27.

Criado-Perez, Caroline. 2019. *Invisible Women*. Chatto & Windus.

Diaz, Sarah. 2020. Science, Technology, and Gender. In *Companion to Women's and Gender Studies*, Ed. Nancy A. Naples. John Wiley & Sons: 111–137.

Dodgson, Lindsay. 2020. The Entrepreneur Who Coined the Term 'FemTech' Founded a Period Tracking App that's Helping Women Understand and Accept Their Bodies. *Insider*. https://www.insider.com/founder-of-clue-ida-tin-coined-the-term-femtech-2020-6.

FemTech Collective Market Report. 2021. www.femtechcollective.com.

FemTech Industry Landscape Overview. FemTech Analytics. December 2021. https://www.femtech.health/femtech-overview-q4-2021.

Figueroa, Caroline A, Tiffany Luo, Adrian Aguilera, and Courtney R Lyles. 2021. The Need for Feminist Intersectionality in Digital Health. *The Lancet* 3: 526–533. https://www.thelancet.com/action/showPdf?pii=S2589-7500%2821%2900118-7.

FitBit. 2022. https://www.fitbit.com/global/uk/home.

Garmin. 2022. https://www.garmin.com/en-GB/.

Hailu, Ruth. 2019. Fitbits and Other Wearables May Not Accurately Track Heart Rates in People of Color. *StatNews*. https://www.statnews.com/2019/07/24/fitbit-accuracy-dark-skin/.

Haraway, Donna. 2003. *The Companion Species Manifesto: Dogs, People, and Significant Otherness*. Prickly Paradigm Press.

Hayes, Tyler. 2014. What's Inside a Fitness Tracker Anyway? *Digital Trends*. https://www.digitaltrends.com/wearables/whats-inside-fitness-tracker-anyway/.

Henriksen, et al. 2018. Using Fitness Trackers and Smartwatches to Measure Physical Activity in Research: Analysis of Consumer Wrist-Worn Wearables. *Journal of Medical Internet Research* 20 (3) https://www.jmir.org/2018/3/e110/.

Heywood, Debbie. 2021. "'Femtech' – getting Data Protection Right in Health Apps." *Taylor Wessing*. https://www.taylorwessing.com/en/interface/2021/femtech-and-issues-around-digitalhealth-products/dl-femtech-getting-data-protection-right-in-health-apps.

Hill, Charlotte. 2015. Wearables—the Future of Biometric Technology? *Biometric Technology Today* 8. https://doi.org/10.1016/S0969-4765(15)30138-7.

Horton, Adrian. 2021. Chris Noth Accused of Sexual Assault by Two Women. *The Guardian*. https://www.theguardian.com/tv-and-radio/2021/dec/16/chris-noth-sexual-assault-accusations-women.

Kearney, Richard. 2019. Double Hospitality Between Word and Touch. *Journal for Continental Philosophy of Religion* 1. https://doi.org/10.116 3/25889613-00101005.

Kristeva, Julia. 1991. *Strangers to Ourselves*. Columbia University Press.

Lashkari, Cashmere. 2019. Types of Sensors in Wearable Fitness Trackers. *NewsMedical Life Sciences*. https://www.news-medical.net/health/Types-of-sensors-in-wearable-fitness-trackers.aspx.

Liedtke, Michael. 2018. Apple to Tutor Women in Tech in Bid to Diversify Industry. *Phys.org*. https://phys.org/news/2018-11-apple-women-tech-diversify-industry.html.

Lovett, Laura. 2018. A Closer Look at Fitbit's New Feature for Women. *MobiHealthNews*. https://www.mobihealthnews.com/content/closer-look-fitbits-new-feature-women.

Lupton, Deborah. 2016. *The Quantified Self*. Wiley.

———. 2017. Feeling Your Data: Touch and Making Sense of Personal Digital Data. *New Media & Society* 19 (10). https://doi.org/10.1177/146144 4817717515.

Mori, Masahiro. 1970. The Uncanny Valley. *IEEE Robotics and Automation Magazine*. Trans. Karl F. MacDorman and Norri Kageki. https://ieeexplore.ieee.org/stamp/stamp.jsp?arnumber=6213238.

Movano. 2022. https://movanohealth.com/.

Murray, Rheana. 2015. Will this Smart Sports Bra Replace Your Usual Fitness Tracker? *Today.com*. https://www.womeninretail.com/cool-tech-this-smart-bra-can-replace-your-fitness-tracker/.

N.a. 2020a. No Body's Business But Mine: How Menstruation Apps Are Sharing Your Data. *Privacy International*. https://www.privacyinternational.org/long-read/3196/no-bodys-business-mine-how-menstruations-apps-are-sharing-your-data.

———. 2020b. Tips and Tricks to Monitor Your health Using Garmin. *Garmin.com*. https://www.garmin.com/en-US/blog/fitness/tips-tricks-to-monitor-your-health-using-garmin/.

———. 2022a. Carnal. *Merriam Webster Dictionary*. https://www.merriam-webster.com/dictionary/carnal.

———. 2022b. UltraHuman Ring. Kickstarter. https://www.kickstarter.com/projects/ultrahuman/ultrahuman-ring-decode-your-metabolism.

Ōura. 2022. Ōura Health. https://ouraring.com/.

Pedersen, Isabel, and Andrew Illiadis, eds. 2020. *Embodied Computing: Wearables, Implantables, Embeddables, Ingestibles*. MIT Press.

Plan International. 2021. https://plan-international.org/.

Ravetto-Biagioli, Kriss. 2019. Self-Uncanny. In *Digital Uncanny*. Oxford University Press.

Reid, Melanie. 2019. Review: Invisible Women: Exposing Data Bias in a World Designed for Men by Caroline Criado Perez—it's a Man's World and Women Don't Fit. *The Sunday Times*. https://www.thetimes.co.uk/article/review-invisible-women-exposing-data-bias-in-a-world-designed-for-men-by-caroline-criado-perez-its-a-mans-world-and-women-dont-fit-rlxw8dl3m.

Rosas, Celia. 2019. The Future Is Femtech: Privacy and Data Security Issues Surrounding Femtech Applications. *Hastings Business Law Journal* 15 (2): 319–341.

Sanders, Rachel. 2017. Self-tracking in the Digital Era: Biopower, Patriarchy, and the New Biometric Body Projects. *Body & Society* 23 (1). https://doi.org/10.1177/1357034X1666036.

Schüll, Natasha. 2016. Tracking. In *Experience*, ed. C. Jones. MIT Press.

Serrano, Julia. 2007. *Whipping girl: A Transsexual Woman on Sexism and the Scapegoating of Femininity*.

Simpson, David. 2013. *Romanticism and the Question of the Stranger*. University of Chicago Press.

Singer, Natalie. 2021. Flo Settles F.T.C. Charges of Misleading Users on Privacy. *New York Times*. https://www.nytimes.com/2021/01/13/business/flo-privacy.html.

Stacey, Jackie, and Sarah Ahmed. 2001. Introduction: Dermographies. In *Thinking Through the Skin*. Routledge.

Taylor. Dan. 2015. Whoops: Apple Watch May Not Work for Black People. *National Monitor*. http://natmonitor.com/2015/04/30/whoops-apple-watch-may-not-work-for-black-people/.

Thomas, Jenny. 2021. FemTech has a Key Part to Play in Women's Health Strategy. *Digital Health London*. https://www.digitalhealth.net/2021/06/femtech-has-a-key-part-to-play-in-womenshealth-strategy/.

Tiffany, Kaitlyn. 2018. Period-tracking Apps are Not for Women. *Vox.com*. https://www.vox.com/the-goods/2018/11/13/18079458/menstrual-tracking-surveillance-glow-clue-apple-health.

Wetsman, Nicole. 2022. Light Sensors on Wearables Struggle with Dark Skin and Obesity. *The Verge*. https://www.theverge.com/2022/1/21/22893133/apple-fitbit-heart-rate-sensor-skin-tone-obesity.

Wissinger, Elizabeth. 2017. Wearable Tech, Bodies, and Gender. *Sociology Compass* 11 (11). https://doi.org/10.1111/soc4.12514.

Zwart, Hub. 2017. 'Extimate' Technologies and Techno-Cultural Discontent: A Lacanian Analysis of Pervasive Gadgets. *Techné: Research in Philosophy and Technology* 21 (1). https://doi.org/10.5840/techne20174560.

CHAPTER 6

Conclusion: Eating the Other and Hacking Hospitality

Eating the Other

In late 2017, the Food and Drug Administration in the US approved what is thought to be the first ingestible sensor technology. Colloquially known as the "digital pill," the company Abilify MyCite was developed as a solution to patients forgetting to take their medication. Specifically targeted at those with mental health conditions such as schizophrenia and bipolar disorder, Abilify also contains a small sensor that, when ingested, can relay information via Bluetooth regarding whether or not a patient is adhering to dosage instructions (Farr 2017). Users must also wear a patch that records additional information such as rest and step counts and can also elect to upload their own data such as mood and sleep patterns to the accompanying app for a more holistic vision of their mental health.

One advertisement banner on the Abilify MyCite homepage shows a man sitting on the edge of his bed. He appears to be in his late 20s to early 30s and is non-white. The text overlaid next to him read: "Is the ABILIFY MYCITE System the right fit for you?" and includes a button below to "Find out" along with the small text at the bottom of the image that declares this is "not a real patient" (Abilify MyCite, 2022). The man sits on an unmade bed, in what appear to be pyjamas or similar "house clothes" (i.e. sweatpants and a t-shirt). Behind him is a room in disarray—clothes strewn across the floor and spilling out of an overturned laundry basket,

L. A. Balfour, *The Digital Future of Hospitality*,
https://doi.org/10.1007/978-3-031-24563-3_6

towels hanging on doors and doorknobs, half-open drawers, and a broken set of venetian blinds—drawn closed even though a few select rays of sun that streak across the room suggest it is a nice day outside. The bedside lampshade is crooked and a lone phone charging cord snakes across the bed, with no phone attached. The man is unshaven (though the beard and goatee seem intentional and fairly well-kept) and he seems to be a construction or safety worker of some kind, evidenced by the steel-toed boots, fluorescent vest, hard hat, and ear protection that are visible in the room.

In many ways, the ad resembles that of a conventional mental health prescription product. Accompanying messages outside the frame dictate safety information and side effects, and helpful infographics explain just how the system works. What is different about this product is its promotion as an explicitly digital tool, combining the familiarity of a small prescription pill with the cutting-edge and still-emerging technology of ingestible sensors. Indeed, Abilify MyCite takes the intimacy and interiority of wearable technologies one step further, beyond the biometrics of touch and directly into the digestive tract. In his co-edited volume *Embodied Computing* (with Isabel Pedersen), Andrew Illiadis (2020) refers to smart pills as a form of "*visceral* computing (computing happening inside the body)." While this perhaps sounds like the stuff of science fiction, it is an instructive way of viewing the body, not simply in relation to computers but the body-as-computer. Moreover, thinking about ingestion as an everyday, and often banal practice, lends a certain degree of familiarity to the smart pill. We think nothing of swallowing a paracetamol for a headache or an antihistamine during allergy season. Moreover, to speak of ingestible technologies is to speak of eating itself. In this way, Deborah Lupton's thoughts on eating the digital seem unquestionably apt. Lupton writes: "how we might begin to theorise the liveliness of digital data in the context of our own vitality, highlighting the relationality and sociality that connect them" (2016). In other words, the smart pill is not just another pill; it is "lively" and can be thought of as a welcome of the stranger in both the digestive and figurative sense. Using food terminology, both ingestion and expulsion are often used as metaphors for (in) hospitality towards the other, and indeed, the self. We might also recall the adage "you are what you eat" as a way of rethinking identity and defining the borders of self and other. So what does it mean to "eat" data and, by extension, to become data as data becomes us? Lupton (2016) continues:

[T]he human subject may be conceptualised as both data-ingesting and data-emitting in an endless cycle of generating data, bringing the data into the self, generating yet more data. Data are absorbed into the body/self and then become new data that flow out of the body/self into the digital data economy. The data-eating/emitting subject, therefore, is not closed off but is open to taking in and letting out digital data.

Such thinking brings us back to the notion not only of the bionic body and biomechanics but also of transplant and the figure of incorporation that operate alongside like new organs or mechanical limbs, data not only grows, but learns within us, and vice versa. In his article "The Law of Hospitality," Julian Pitt-Rivers describes incorporation as the successful movement from guest to permanence. In his words, "while the mode of permanent incorporation solidifies in time, the status of guest evaporates" (2012). In *Hospitality in a Time of Terror* (2017), I discussed the phenomenon of incorporation in the context of dust from the fall of the Twin Towers in 2001. This dust, a pulverized composite of metal, concrete, and (most likely) human remains, is simultaneously architectural and biological, the implications of which are profound when we remember the frequency with which this dust was inhaled into the lungs of New Yorkers for weeks following the 9/11 attacks. In this analysis, I discussed "the ways in which hospitality paradoxically succeeds and fails on a model of incorporation. [Dust] suggests an unconditional welcome of strangers but also an incorporation that levels the other to a figure of familiarity, and a figure whose alterity is potentially negated when incorporated by the host" (Balfour 2017). Six years following the attacks, author Don DeLillo wrote biological incorporation into his novel *Falling Man* by narrating the experience of a fictional survivor who discovers that his body has incorporated bits of flesh from the victims (and possibly hijackers) who were near to him at the moment the plane impacted the tower. His doctor calls this "organic shrapnel," when "fragments of flesh and bone come flying outward with such force and velocity that they get wedged, they get trapped in the body of anyone who's in striking range" (DeLillo 2007). The critical point here is that while the life of the victim or hijacker has been extinguished, those extracted bits of flesh go on to live in their new host. I raise this scene not only to reinforce hospitality as ethics of embeddedness, but also to draw attention back to the ways in which the ingestible, whether digital or organic, is *material*. Significantly, it also reminds us that incorporation, however hospitable, is most often unwilled and uninvited. Indeed, some-times, even in life-saving scenarios, it can be a failure.

And so, we must also contend with the reality of unsuccessful incorpo-ration, when such absorption or embeddedness fails and remains defiantly other. The raised bumps or edges of a skin graft, the outright rejection of a transplanted organ, the uncanny sensation of a foreign limb, and the autoimmune: these are the figures of refusal that speak to the body's instinct to immunize itself against a foreign other. The British Society for Immunology describes this threat of rejection:

> The complex mechanisms of immunity, which under normal circumstances work to identify foreign microbes and direct the immune system to destroy them, pose a significant barrier to successful transplantation. Rejection of a transplant occurs in instances where the immune system identifies the trans-plant as foreign, triggering a response that will ultimately destroy the trans-planted organ or tissue. (2017)

Immunology and hospitality seem to share the same language here, alter-nating between welcome and expulsion and bringing the ethics of incor-poration into embodied and posthuman focus, particularly in consideration of biomechanical networks within the host body. To receive a foreign body into one's own is to accept this risk, between welcome or rejection, hospitality or hostility. For Elina Staikou (2014), "transplantation is thought here in terms that waver between vulnerability and enhancement and it is inevitably conjoined with the motif of the self's immunity, what would normally resist the intruder and what must be overcome in trans-plantation." Indeed, in the 1980s the study of immunology was referred to as "the science of self-nonself discrimination" (Pradeu 2020). In using this phrase, Thomas Pradeu embraces what he calls "the philosophy of immunology" as a way of contending with the biological realities of self and non-self-living together (in this case, in the body). He estimates, moreover, that "a human host, for example, is made up of as many bacte-rial cells as its genetically self cells" (Pradeu 2020). We might think of referring to hospitality in a similar way and thinking about the immune system as a defence against a foreign other reminds us of the degree to which hospitality ultimately forsakes or flourishes through incorporation and what Derrida emphatically argues is necessarily autoimmunitary. Derrida describes autoimmunity as "that strange behaviour where a living being, in quasi-suicidal fashion, 'itself' works to destroy its own protection, to immunize itself against its 'own' immunity" (in Borradori 2003). Autoimmunity thus describes the failure of immunity before the self is actually threatened. But this is a necessary failure if hospitality is to succeed.

Along these lines, there is perhaps one figure of digital life that so readily recalls the paradox of hospitality and brings these deep digital anxieties into focus. But what seems so obvious and routine (if frustrating) in the computer world is perhaps hospitality's most enduring metaphor. I am speaking here of contamination, of the parasite and, in the context of our digital lives, the computer virus in particular.[1] There is no hospitality without this threat. One must not just be okay with but must *welcome* contamination—an openness to contamination *before* contact. What better figure of this than the computer? The technologies we use today may be new but Derrida in particular has always likened contagion to a kind of technological process: "The virus is in part a parasite that destroys, that introduces disorder into communication. Even from the biological standpoint, this is what happens with a virus; it derails a mechanism of the communicational type, its coding and decoding" (in Mitchell 2005). Viral metaphors have also been readily applied as a threat in popular culture and political and technological discourses. Outside of conversations around health, we are more likely to use the word "viral" to describe the spreadability of media, and the speed and reach of popular videos and memes. And while "meme" might seem like a recent phenomenon, its etymology is actually drawn from immunology. The term was, in fact, coined by Richard Dawkins in 1976 and was understood by Dawkins as the cultural equivalent to the gene: "Just as genes propagate themselves in the gene pool by leaping from body to body via sperm or eggs, so memes propagate themselves in the meme pool by leaping from brain to brain via a process which, in the broad sense, can be called imitation" (Green and Jenkins 2014). Meme, of course, is borrowed here from *mimesis*. Whether from brain to brain or from computer to computer, the viral meme demands consideration as a serious figure in thinking about what it means to welcome the stranger in an age of global health panic *and* technological uncertainty.

---

[1] Indeed, virology in general has become a defining concern of contemporary life as we continue to grapple with the effects of the COVID-19 pandemic. There has never been a more apt time to consider a social history of "the virus" and "the viral."

The virus also has other significant cultural meanings, especially in the wake of the COVID-19 pandemic, that have explicit implications for hospitality in both the philosophical and geopolitical sense, not to mention the proliferation of physical lockdowns, effectively cutting off strangers of all kinds. In particular, the notion of a disease or parasite that multiplies within the body, the body politic—or, I would add, the device—and attacks those internal defence systems often becomes a ready-made symbol for guests that do not *arrive* so much as they *emerge* from within the host body—what we now might think of as the "server."

Whether body or machine—though surely the body has always been a machine that learns and self-preserves—and given the body's instincts to reject what is foreign, something else must be added to the encounter, something that initiates the autoimmune and "enables an exposure to the other, to what and to who comes" (Derrida 2005). In a successful transplant, for example, the success is "not the surgical procedure itself but the use of immunosuppressor drugs in order to protect from graft immunological reactivity and rejection" (Staikou 2014). In other words, the moment of hospitality is the incorporation of the immunosuppressant and not the incorporation of the foreign organ, implant, or other agent. This, importantly, is a hospitality brought *through* (bio)technology, not in spite of it. Beyond transplantation and in the now ever-present discourses of virology, we see an immunitary process at work in the vaccine, and in the digital landscape, by anti-virus software and cybersecurity, and biometric surveillance. These are the strategies of inhospitality that reject the foreigner and come in by way of viral panic, hacking, and border security. And so, looking back at the examples this monograph brings forth, we can see an autoimmunitary process at work, from the lines of code that arrive already embedded in the android host body, to the pre-loaded software of Siri and Alexa that pre-emptively conditions their response, to the algorithms of Airbnb that predetermine who can be a host or guest at all, and finally in the predictive health metrics of wearable tech. If, then, hospitality is philosophical and digital, it is also political.

HACKING HOSPITALITY

This book has endeavoured to revive and reclaim hospitality in the context of digital life and emergent technology. Along the way, I have moved from the fictional, external, and representational to the internal and deeply intimate. Indeed, Chap. 2 cast a glance towards the fictional screen relationships between humans and android hosts as a way of initiating a series of questions about hospitality and violence to and of the more-than-human. That lens then turned increasingly inward, from relations with virtual agents in domestic space to the platform intimacies of the gig economy and hospitality between strangers. In Chap. 5, the analysis went beneath the surface of the self, uncovering the most intimate of all and the complex hospitality of body-data relations. The sense of shrinking proximity has been intentional and what began as perhaps an indictment of hospitality in the digital era has brought hospitality closer than ever. It has also exposed the need to rethink hospitality alongside pressing concerns about data, privacy, and the relationship between bodies and technology.

And so I want to return once more to the UltraHuman ring discussed in Chap. 5, not to review the role of wearables in discourses of self-estrangement, but to consider where hospitality might go from here. Indeed, UltraHuman seems, on the surface, to offer a new smart fitness product but inadvertently draws our attention to a new figure of hospitality and reanimates ethics of welcome by appealing to the outsiders potentially left out of the biometric tracking industry. Through their product, they seek to energize, along with athletes and fitness lovers, "the world's largest community of *biohackers*" (UltraHuman 2022, my emphasis). Such a decision is perhaps risky; rather than adhere to the more conventional promises of medical and scientific accuracy, or promise compatibility with one's GP or chemist, the UltraHuman ring uses a new language of health, adopting phrases such as "predictive insights," "holistic," and "fitness ecosystem." Such language is aimed at a particular community—those who subscribe to more unorthodox or do-it-yourself mechanisms for health enhancement (see Marr 2021; Hamblin 2019). Writing for *The Verge*, Victoria Song finds a similar subversive vein to UltraHuman's promises, describing it as a smart ring that "aims to 'hack' your metabolism" (2022). Not only is the notion of hacking a disruption to traditional modes of consumer capitalism, it also conjures ideas of unlawful entry or even invasion that are, once again, eerily resonant with hospitality. Most reading this will be familiar with the concept of hacking; aside from individual concerns about malware and stolen pin codes, phenomena such as Wikileaks and Anonymous have brought hacking to the mainstream and to news headlines globally. For Mariele Kauffman, the relationship between hackers and their primary site of engagement is a complicated one. She describes: "To most hackers, the Internet is a space that they partly built themselves, which creates a sense of ownership. At the same time, it is also an infrastructure that has traceability and surveillance deeply engrained in its architecture" (2020). Much like hospitality itself, hacking is a concept fraught with contradiction but one that offers some useful figures for reanimating the philosophy of hospitality in such a way that it might contend with the pressing social, cultural, and political challenges of our digital present and future.

In a 1986 issue of the hacking e-zine *Phrack*, Loyd Blankenship published "The Conscience of a Hacker" under his pseudonym "The Mentor." Colloquially known as "The Hacker Manifesto," The Mentor's declaration gestures to several figures of hospitality and human-computer co-dependence, not the least of which is a direct nod to communities of unconditional welcome. It is worth reposting a short, abridged version here:

> *I am a hacker, enter my world...*
>
> *I made a discovery today. I found a computer. Wait a second, this is cool. It does what I want it to. If it makes a mistake, it's because I screwed it up. Not because it doesn't like me...*
>
> *Or feels threatened by me...*
>
> *This is our world now... the world of the electron and the switch, the beauty of the baud. We make use of a service already existing without paying for what could be dirt-cheap if it wasn't run by profiteering gluttons, and you call us criminals. We explore... and you call us criminals. We seek after knowledge... and you call us criminals. We exist without skin color, without nationality, without religious bias... and you call us criminals. You build atomic bombs, you wage wars, you murder, cheat, and lie to us and try to make us believe it's for our own good, yet we're the criminals.*
>
> *Yes, I am a criminal. My crime is that of curiosity. My crime is that of judging people by what they say and think, not what they look like. My crime is that of outsmarting you, something that you will never forgive me for.*
>
> *I am a hacker, and this is my manifesto. You may stop this individual, but you can't stop us all... after all, we're all alike.* (The Mentor 1986)

The Mentor's "Manifesto" begins with an invitation. It beckons the reader into the world of hacking—a space that is perhaps not entirely safe for either host or guest. What follows next is an interesting claim that he possesses power over technology, and an ability to manipulate it, yet he simultaneously presents it as a non-threat. In other words, the technology isn't the problem here, nor is it to be feared. The statement "this is our world now" suggests that while initially an invitation, the presence of the hacker is now more of an inhabitation, even an occupation; it is an arrival (without invitation) into the world of the "electron and the switch" and a disruption to the (host) network. The Mentor also directly addresses the reader. This is not a manifesto for other hackers; rather it is a declaration of intent, directed at "you" (the reader, the glutton, the capitalist). Significantly, The Mentor avoids all attempts at being categorized, identified, or individualized. Efforts to make him (and other hackers) foreign by calling them "criminals" is thwarted by the manifesto's claims to community, shared occupation of the digital world, and a rejection of recognition (including that based on race, religion, or nationality). Ultimately "The Conscience of a Hacker" invokes curiosity not as a crime but as an ethic. A welcome to whatever arrives, and an openness without judgement. The final claim that "we're all alike" once more resists individualization and the distinction between self and other. Indeed, as Kauffman argues, "subjects who self-identify as hackers and analyse the many ways in which they answer online surveillance without abandoning the Internet as such…hacking is a science of staying curious which is also a starting point for critique" (2020). Can we think of hospitality in the same way? Could we possibly rethink its purpose, potentials, and new spaces without abandoning it? Kauffman suggests that "hacking would then become the "critical, creative, reflective and subversive use of technology that allows creating new meanings" (2020). Surely, we can hack hospitality as a way of critiquing its more rigid structures while keeping the spirit of welcome alive. No longer a welcome unto death but an expanding of curiosity and critique that proceeds, once more in David L. Clark's words (in Redfield 2009), "as if peace were possible"?

In 1975, one of the first definitions of hacking was offered by a team developing a glossary for computer programming at MIT. In this document, aptly named "The Jargon File," they suggested a few definitions for "hacker" that suggest a revisionist rather than malicious relationship with technology and its users. These definitions include "1. A person who enjoys exploring the details of programmable systems and how to stretch their capabilities; 2. One who enjoys programming rather than just theorizing about programming; [and] 7. One who enjoys the intellectual challenge of creatively overcoming or circumventing limitations" ("Hacker," 1975). I am not suggesting that we completely forsake thinking on hospitality as we have known it thus far. Its tensions, entanglements, and contradictions remain important, as does its ethical horizon as an unconditional welcome of the other, any other, even if that horizon remains distant, or in Derrida's words "a venir" (in Borradori 2003). What I am suggesting is a "hacked" hospitality—one that, according to MIT's definition, sees its capabilities stretched, moves beyond theory, and overcomes and circumvents limitations. A "hacked" hospitality means welcoming the surprise encounter in the form of digital strangers who are already a part of ourselves and stretch the limits of ourselves. Hacking hospitality means refusing to distinguish between human and not and seeing the digital as a co-dependent relation rather than either slave or adversary. It means forsaking personal and political immunity and overwhelming the system that sustains borders and biopower. Hacking hospitality, at the very least, is a response as creative (and potentially as disruptive) as the Trojan horse, understood now as a form of malware whereby a user is duped into opening an email attachment or clicking through on a link disguised as something harmless. The term, of course, also elicits the mythic wooden horse sent by the Greeks to the city of Troy as a gift, only to spill forth an army of concealed warriors when inside the walls, where they lay siege to the city. Hospitality itself is still under siege but perhaps the most surprising and unexpected figures of strangeness that arrive not in a wooden horse but in the lines of code that now define our contemporary existence offer up a chance to think beyond the impossible and remind us of the necessity of holding hospitality intact. Both as a figure of failed welcome and of subterfuge, the Trojan horse conjures a new digital stranger at the same time as it returns us, perhaps fittingly, to the Greeks, but through metaphor rather than violence. It returns us to the rituals of hospitality embedded in antiquity if only to write a new history of welcoming the stranger—now one of human-computer relationality, ecological vitality, cellular co-dependence, non-violence, and affirmative politics. In other words, an account of hospitality for our digital future.

References

Balfour, Lindsay. 2017. *Hospitality in a Time of Terror: Strangers at the Gate.* Rowman & Littlefield.

Borradori, Giovanna. 2003. *Philosophy in a Time of Terror: Dialogues with Jürgen Habermas and Jacques Derrida.* University of Chicago Press.

DeLillo, Don. 2007. *Falling Man.* Scribner.

Derrida, Jacques. 2005. The Principle of Hospitality. *Parallax* 11 (1). https://doi.org/10.1080/1353464052000321056.

Farr, Christina. 2017. The First 'Digital Pill' Has Just been Approved—Here's How it Could Revolutionize Health Care. *CNBCNews*. https://www.cnbc.com/2017/11/14/what-is-a-digital-pill.html.

Green, Joshua, and Henry Jenkins. 2014. Spreadable Media: How Audiences Create Value and Meaning in a Networked Economy. In *The Handbook of Media Audiences*, ed. Virginia Nightingale. John Wiley and Sons.

Hamblin, James. 2019. 7 Biohacks to Master Before Worrying About other Biohacks. *The Atlantic*. https://www.theatlantic.com/health/archive/2019/03/top-biohacks/584584/.

Illiadis, Andrew. 2020. Computer Guts and Swallowed Sensors: Ingestibles made Palatable in an Era of Embodied Computing. In *Embodied Computing*, eds. Isabel Pedersen and Andrew Illiadis, 1–20. MIT Press.

Kauffman, Mariele. 2020. Hacking Surveillance. *First Monday* 25 (5). https://journals.uic.edu/ojs/index.php/fm/article/view/10006/9419.

Lupton, Deborah. 2016. Digital Companion Species and Eating Data: Implications for Theorising Digital Data-human assemblages. *Big Data & Society*. https://doi.org/10.1177/2053951715619947.

Marr, Bernard. 2021. What's Biohacking? All you Need to Know About the Latest Craze. *Forbes*. https://www.forbes.com/sites/bernardmarr/2021/02/26/whats-biohacking-all-you-need-to-know-about-the-latest-health-craze/?sh=2d661e585d76.

Mitchell, W.J.T. 2005. Picturing Terror: Derrida's Autoimmunity. *Cardozo Law Review* 27 (2). https://doi.org/10.1086/511494.

N.a. 2017. Transplant Immunology. British Society for Immunology. Brief. https://www.immunology.org/policy-and-public-affairs/briefings-and-position-statements/transplant-immunology.

———. 2022. UltraHuman Ring. *Kickstarter*. https://www.kickstarter.com/projects/ultrahuman/ultrahuman-ring-decode-your-metabolism.

Pitt-Rivers, Julian. 2012. The Law of Hospitality. *HAU: Journal of Ethnographic Theory* 2 (1) https://doi.org/10.14318/hau2.1.022.

Pradeu, Thomas. 2020. *Philosophy of Immunology*. Cambridge University Press.

Redfield, Marc. 2009. *The Rhetoric of Terror: Reflections on 9/11 and the War on Terror*. New York: Fordham University Press.

Staikou, Elina. 2014. Putting in the Graft. *Derrida Today* 7 (2). https://www.jstor.org/stable/10.2307/48616430.

The Mentor. 1986. The Conscience of a Hacker. *Phrack* 1 (7). http://phrack.org/issues/7/3.html.

Index[1]

[1] Note: Page numbers followed by 'n' refer to notes.

Ingram Content Group UK Ltd.
Milton Keynes UK
UKHW021145220623
423860UK00004B/170

9 783031 245626